Doctor Van Fleet's

amazing new

"non-glue-food"

diet

JAMES K. VAN FLEET, D. C.

Parker Publishing Company
West Nyack, New York

© 1974 by
James K. Van Fleet

*All rights reserved. No part of this
book may be reproduced in any form
or by any means, without permission
in writing from the publisher.*

Library of Congress Cataloging in Publication Data

Van Fleet, James K
   Doctor Van Fleet's amazing new "non-glue food" diet.

   1. Reducing diets. I. Title. [DNLM: 1. Diet,
Reducing. WD212 V252d 1974]
RM222.2.V28   613.2'5   74-3495
ISBN 0-13-216978-9

Printed in the United States of America

To my Family

What this book will do for you

The "Non-Glue-Food" Diet will help you lose *all* your excess fat quickly, safely, easily, and permanently, no matter how much you weigh now.

If you have 20 pounds or less of excess fat to lose, you'll be able to get rid of it at the rate of two or three pounds each week. In no more than ten weeks — perhaps even less — you can lose all your excess fat and be down to your ideal weight painlessly, easily, and without any effort whatever.

If you have more than 20 pounds of excess fat to lose, you'll be able to get rid of four or five pounds each week with a slightly different version of my original non-glue-food diet.

Naturally, the more pounds you need to lose, the longer it will take; but you can still get down to your ideal weight in a short time without any problems at all. I know this is possible, for I've seen it happen so many times before with my patients. Let me recall just a few of them for you.

For instance, there was Everett, a gentleman in his mid-sixties who weighed 226 pounds when he came to see me. He's down to 165 now on my non-glue-food diet.

And then there was Margie, the unhappy 17-year-old who weighed 168 pounds when she came to my office. She got rid of 48 pounds by following my non-glue-food diet and by using my non-glue-food meal-planning guide. She was elected the homecoming queen at her high school (her figure had a lot to do with it).

And how could I forget Homer? He was one of the fattest patients I've ever had. He weighed in at 286 pounds when he first came to see me. He was so fat he used to sit on two restaurant stools at the same time. After a year on my non-glue-food diet, Homer had lost 91 pounds. He tipped the scales at 195 pounds and attained his ideal weight a little later.

I especially remember Joyce for she had a special weight problem. Every time she had dieted before, she lost fat in the wrong places — her breasts, for example, while her tummy remained full and flabby. But on the non-glue-food diet with its vital body-tissue-building foods, she was able this time to reduce in the right places.

I can think of hundreds of others I could mention here, but you'll meet a lot of them later on. Besides, right now I want to tell you about some of the —

Benefits you'll gain

The benefits you'll gain from getting rid of your excess fat are tremendous. I'll not cover them all here, but I will mention just a few of the most important ones for you.

1. You'll have more energy, more vitality, more pep and go-power.

2. Your complexion will be clear; your hair will shine.

3. You'll be free from a grim collection of aches and pains.

4. You'll be "regular" without laxatives; your digestion will improve.

5. You'll not be nervous and high strung; you'll even sleep better.

6. If you're a woman, you'll be mistaken for your daughter.

7. You won't have to make excuses to anyone for your figure, even when you wear a swimsuit.

8. You can be the envy of your "plump" friends.

9. You'll look and feel at least five to ten years younger.

10. Your sex life will improve dramatically.

How the non-glue-food diet makes it easy for you to get rid of your excess fat

1. *Your individual non-glue-food diet is specifically tailored to the number of pounds you need to lose.* If you have 20 pounds or less to get rid of, the first version of the non-glue-food diet is for you. If you have from 20 to 40 pounds to lose, the second version is the one to use. If you are more than 40 pounds overweight, you can use the third version of the non-glue-food diet.

2. The non-glue-food diet eliminates the cause of your excess fat. Other diets generally do not.

3. On the non-glue-food diet you lose ugly, unwanted fat — not just weight.

4. Your weight loss will be permanent.

5. On the non-glue-food diet you avoid only the glue-foods that make you fat.

6. When you don't eat the glue-foods, hunger stays away longer.

7. You don't have to starve yourself because you are never hungry.

8. Generally speaking, you can eat all the meat, poultry, fish and seafood, dairy products, and fresh fruits and vegetables you want.

9. You can satisfy your sweet tooth and not get fat.

10. You don't have to use willpower on this diet.

11. You'll not become exhausted, worn-out, fatigued, irritable, and nervous, nor will you lose all your energy on the non-glue-food diet.

12. You can maintain this diet indefinitely without any danger to your health. In fact, as you lose your excess fat, you'll gain back your health.

The non-glue-food diet is pleasant and easy. And best of all, it really works for you. It gets rid of your ugly excess fat.

The Author

Contents

What this book will do for you •   7

1. How to motivate yourself to reduce and get rid of your excess fat •   19

Desire is the first law of success in whatever you set out to do   21
You must always reach this point before you can become
    successful   22
The head never hears 'til the heart has listened   25
How to find the real reason you want to get rid of your excess fat   26
How to stimulate your subconscious mind to work for you   28
"Doctor, how much should I really weigh?"   29
How to establish a reasonable and attainable weight goal   30
How to use inches instead of pounds as your goal   32
You don't need willpower to get rid of your excess fat   34
Here's how to forget your excess fat problem so you can solve it   36
Why you're going to succeed this time   37

2. How the non-glue-food diet works when other diets fail •   39

        Section I: Why the Low-Calorie Diet Does Not Work for
                  Permanent Weight Loss
The law of thermodynamics applies to human physiology   40
The low-calorie diet and that tired feeling   40
The low-calorie diet and muscle-tissue loss   41

The low-calorie diet and regained weight   42

Section II: How to Select Foods That Help You Lose Weight
Without Regrets

How my term "glue-foods" evolved   44

Glue-food is the real reason people get fat   44

The author's experience   45

Glue-food consumption is the major cause of overweight   46

The test for glue-food   47

How glue-foods work to make you fat   48

Most fat people are foodaholics   51

Why don't glue-foods make everybody fat?   52

Section III: What You've Always Wanted to Know About
Glue-Foods Causing Overweight

Proteins are important non-glue-foods   57

Fats are also non-glue-foods   57

Natural carbohydrates are non-glue-foods   62

11 reasons why the non-glue-food diet will work for you   64

3. **How to use the non-glue-food diet to lose all your excess fat
no matter how much you weigh now ●   67**

The non-glue-food diet is neither a crash diet nor a starvation diet   70

Benefits you'll gain   71

Section I: How to Lose Two or Three Pounds Each Week

Eliminate all the glue-foods from your diet   72

Eat all the protein foods you want   73

Eat all the fresh, frozen, or canned fruits and vegetables you want   75

All types of potato servings put on weight   77

For even faster weight loss results, use the three-to-one rule   79

Drink all you want of these beverages   80

Avoid or limit these beverages   81

Dressings and garnishes you can use freely   82

You can use these condiments for seasoning   82

How to establish a sensible eating pattern as soon as possible   83

How to satisfy your sweet tooth   86

To speed up your fat loss, add polyunsaturated fats to your diet   86

Add multi-vitamin, multi-mineral supplements to your diet 90

What to do about parties and drinking 93

Forget your excess fat problem for 30 days 95

Points to remember 96

Section II: How to Lose Four or Five Pounds Each Week

Your pancreas will now treat some fruits and vegetables as glue-
foods 97

Part 1: How to diet if you have between 20 and 40 pounds to lose 99

Part 2: How to diet if you have more than 40 pounds to lose 105

Part 3: The Eskimo Diet or Caveman's Diet 106

Section III: Here's a Quick Summary of the Non-Glue-Food
Diets in Chapter Three

Section IV: A Bit of Advice Before You Start Your Diet

4. Your non-glue-food meal-planning guide • 117

Section I: Here's Your Basic Meal-Planning Guide if You
Have 20 Pounds or Less to Lose

Section II: Here's Your Basic Meal-Planning Guide if You
Have from 20 to 40 Pounds to Lose

Section III: Here's Your Basic Meal-Planning Guide if You
Have More Than 40 Pounds to Lose

Section IV: Here's Your Basic Meal-Planning Guide for the
Eskimo or Caveman's Diet

Section V: A Selected List of My Favorite Non-Glue-Food
Recipes

5. How the non-glue-food diet can make you more attractive
and increase your sexual powers • 147

Ninety-five percent of all my fat patients have a problem with
sex 148

You'll gain these benefits 149

Sex begins in the dining room—not in the bedroom 150

Why minerals are important for sexual power 161

Why age need not be a barrier to sex 164

6. How the non-glue-food diet can make you look and feel 10 to 20 years younger ●   169

Here's the key to how old you look and feel   169

When your carbohydrate metabolism is abnormal, you will age pre-maturely; you will get old long before your time   170

The non-glue-food diet can make you look and feel much younger   171

You'll gain these benefits   173

How to have a youthful skin and a radiant complexion   174

You can't lose weight by exercise alone   180

Mild exercise is beneficial   181

To stay young at heart, associate with people who think young   181

You can postpone age indefinitely with the non-glue-food diet   184

7. Various health conditions improved by the non-glue-food diet ●   187

Benefits you'll gain   188

Facts and figures about fat people and death   188

In these specific diseases, the death rate is higher in fat people   189

How excess fat affects your health   190

What happens to your heart when you get rid of your excess fat   192

How excess fat affects your blood pressure   193

Arthritis and rheumatism are much worse when you are fat   194

Even your low nagging backache may go away   196

You'll get rid of your indigestion, acid stomach, and heartburn   197

You'll no longer be short of breath   198

Fat people are not jolly all the time   199

The non-glue-food diet can prevent or control diabetes   200

Fat people usually have poor circulation   201

Other conditions usually helped by the non-glue-food diet   202

8. What to do after you reach your weight goal ●   203

Take a picture of your new self   205

Buy yourself a complete new wardrobe   206

Don't eat any more of the glue-foods that got you fat in the first place 206

Don't try to be a social eater 208

Here's a quick summary of easy rules to remember and practice 209

What to do if you go over your three-pound limitation 209

Index • 211

Doctor Van Fleet's

amazing new

"non-glue-food"

diet

1. How to motivate yourself to reduce and get rid of your excess fat

Most people who try to reduce and get rid of their excess fat visualize losing their extra pounds as a final benefit to be gained. But just getting rid of your surplus fat is not a final benefit in itself. That's why people who try to reduce with only that one goal in mind are never motivated strongly enough to get the job done.

Getting rid of your excess fat is a technique in a program that will allow you to reach your true goal and win the specific benefits that you really want to gain.

For instance, losing 20 or 30 pounds of excess fat is a technique you can use to gain the worthwhile benefits of better physical health: having more vigor and vitality and go-power; getting rid of a variety of aches and pains; calming down your palpitating heart; lowering your blood pressure; alleviating constipation; getting rid of itching hemorrhoids; soothing your sore and aching feet, your nagging low backache, and so on.

These physical benefits, which will be yours when you get rid of your excess fat, represent only the beginning of a much better life for you. They will be followed by even more exciting benefits for you to enjoy to the fullest.

Just for example, when you get rid of your shortness of breath, your nagging low backache, your palpitating heart, and the excess lard around your middle, making love with your partner will become a pleasure instead of an obligation and a chore. You can enjoy sex whenever you want to instead of feeling duty bound to do something about it once a week or so.

To cite a recent case, the other day one of my patients said to me, "Doc, our love life is great now. My wife has lost 66 pounds on your non-glue-food diet in 18 weeks and I've dropped 53 pounds in the same length of time. She went from 206 down to 140 and I've gone from 198 to 145. We feel terrific in every respect. We're in our early sixties, as you well know, Doc, and frankly, we gave up sexual relations quite some time ago. We thought we were finished. But now that we've both lost weight, we find that's not true. There's still a lot of life left in both of us. And we owe it all to you and your non-glue-food diet!"

Of course, there are always the psychic benefits to be gained, too. These will furnish additional momentum to get you in gear. Such benefits as respect and admiration from your friends, compliments and extra glances from the opposite sex — especially at the pool — all these can be yours when you get rid of your ugly excess fat.

So don't look at the loss of extra pounds as a final goal in itself. Instead, think of it as a technique you can use to reach your final objective and win the specific health benefits you want to gain for yourself. That way you'll be motivated strongly enough to reduce and get the job done. You'll be able to get rid of your excess fat.

Desire is the first law of success
in whatever you set out to do

"Doctor, I *need* to reduce; I have to lose weight," a fat patient said to me in my office one day.

"I know you need to reduce, Evelyn," I said. "And I could give you a half-dozen good reasons why you should: your high blood pressure, the overload on your heart, your poor circulation and varicose veins, your tendency toward diabetes, maybe even nephritis, kidney failure, or worse. But first, Evelyn, I must ask you this: Do you really *want* to reduce?"

"No, I don't really want to," she said, "but I ought to."

"That's not a good enough reason, Evelyn," I said. "Needing to reduce is not nearly enough incentive for you to do it. Everybody ought to stop smoking cigarettes, for instance, but not everyone does. Only those who really want to quit ever do so.

"It's the same with you, too, Evelyn. Needing to reduce is just not enough to get you to do it. *You'll never succeed in getting rid of your excess fat unless you really want to.* I cannot accept you as a patient nor will I put you on my non-glue-food diet until you actually want to reduce and get rid of your extra pounds.

"So here's what I'd like you to do: I want you to take this little pamphlet home with you and read it. It tells you all about my non-glue-food diet: what it is, how it works, what it will do for you, why it'll do it. I'd like you to read it every day and think about your fat problem for at least a week — longer if necessary. I want you to figure out for yourself *why you really want to get rid of your excess fat.*

"I'll give you one little hint, too, Evelyn. Don't try to give yourself a doctor's reasons for wanting to lose your extra fat. You already know what they are. I've told you and they're not enough. See if you can come up with some emotional reasons that make you burn with desire to reduce — like more attention, more appreciation, more love, more sex from your husband — compliments, respect and admiration from your friends.

"When you know your *real reason for wanting to reduce,* come back and see me. Tell me why it's so important to you to get rid of your excess fat. Then we can go to work to solve your fat problem for you."

Evelyn did succeed; she was able to solve her problem. Once she discovered the real reason she wanted to reduce, she was able to motivate herself to do so. She used my non-glue-food diet and meal-planning guide faithfully and successfully to get rid of all her excess fat. I can truthfully say that Evelyn has been one of the best patients I've ever had because she knew exactly what she wanted.

Why do I handle my fat patients this way? Why don't I just start them right off on my non-glue-food diet? Because I know from long experience that they will not succeed unless they really do want to reduce and lose their excess fat, and unless they actually do know why they're doing it or what their specific benefits will be.

If you can motivate yourself properly to get rid of your excess fat, you'll be able to reduce quickly, safely, easily, and permanently, *because you'll want to — not just because you have to.*

You must always reach this point before you can become successful

"Carl, why is it so many fat people don't want to reduce even when they know it's dangerous to their health to be overweight?" I once asked Carl S.

"Because they haven't reached bottom yet, Doc," Carl replied. "They haven't reached the point where they can no longer stand themselves the way they are. A fat person is like an alcoholic in many ways, Doc. An alcoholic won't stop drinking until he reaches the point where he can no longer stand himself the way he is. When he does reach that point, he'll do something about his alcoholism, but not before.

"A fat person is exactly the same: *he's a foodaholic.* He won't stop eating until he reaches that point of intolerance. I know, Doc; I've been in both places."

Carl is one of my patients — formerly a fat one, now a thin one. He used to tip the scales at 232; now he can only get them up to 173. He has used my non-glue-food diet and my meal-planning guide to reduce successfully and to remain slim, trim, and in excellent health. Carl is also a member of Alcoholics Anonymous and he has been able to apply some of the concepts of AA to his diet program.

If this should seem surprising to you, it might help you to know that a great many other groups of people — Gamblers Anonymous, Fatties Anonymous, Synanon, just to mention a few — have used various principles and procedures of Alcoholics Anonymous to help them solve their own particular problems.

So I have learned much from Carl. I, too, have been able to use certain aspects of AA philosophy to help my fat patients get in the right psychological frame of mind to get rid of their excess fat.

The idea of reaching the point where you can no longer stand yourself the way you are is just one of the methods I've adopted from Alcoholics Anonymous for my non-glue-food diet. I always tell my patients that they must include this idea in their reducing programs.

Just as this is an extremely important step in an alcoholic's return to sobriety and a normal life, so is it an important step in the fat person's return to slimness and a normal, happy life.

If this should happen to you, you'll hit bottom fast, too

Some time ago, a fat, 210-pound woman sat in my office crying as if her heart would break. "Fred made fun of me," she said, sobbing and wiping her eyes. "He laughed at me because I'm so fat!"

"What happened, Lucille?" I asked. "Tell me all about it."

"Well, he was going to his weekly bowling league the other night and I didn't want to stay home alone. But he wouldn't take me along. Said none of the other fellows ever brought their wives.

"We live near the college campus and I was afraid to stay home all by myself. There've been several reports of college girls being raped on their way home at night from the library. Not only that, three houses in our neighborhood have been burglarized recently. So I was scared about staying home alone.

"But Fred just laughed at me as if it were all a big joke. 'You don't have a thing to worry about, Lucille,' he said. 'If anyone ever sees you without your clothes on, he'll forget all about wanting to rape you. He'll be so scared he'll run away as fast as he can!' "

"Don't cry, Lucille," I said. "Could be the best thing that ever happened to you, for underneath all that excess fat you're carrying around, you're really a very beautiful woman. After you get rid of your extra pounds, Fred won't be laughing at you any more. He'll be keeping a jealous eye on you instead. I'll bet he won't leave you at home alone any more at night either."

And I was right. Lucille went from 210 pounds down to 130 on my non-glue-food diet and now looks absolutely stunning. Fred doesn't leave her at home alone any more whenever he goes bowling. Wherever he goes, she goes, and vice-versa.

You see, the average person can tolerate almost any insult, any defeat, any injury, and accept it with some semblance of good grace. But when someone makes fun of him, when someone belittles or ridicules him, well, that's usually the last straw. It's the final insult, the final breaking point that will motivate an individual to do something about the problem — in Lucille's case, her excess fat.

So when someone ridicules you, makes fun of you, or laughs at you for being so fat, don't get upset and feel bad. Thank them instead. It could be the best thing that ever happened to you, too. It could be the turning point in your life that causes you to at last do something to solve your own weight problem.

The head never hears 'til the heart has listened

"Doc, I don't understand myself at all," a 205-pound patient once said to me. "I know I need to lose weight, but I don't want to at all. How do I convince myself to get the job done? What can I do?"

"You're evidently trying to reduce with only your conscious mind, George," I said, "and that won't work. *You must sell your subconscious mind on the idea first.* Then you can lose all your excess fat easily. Let me explain that to you in a little more detail this way.

"You see, George, you have two separate minds. One is the mind of your head — *the intellectual conscious mind.* It uses cold, hard logic and reasoning to make its decisions. It *thinks* about what you should do and why you ought to do it.

"The other one is the mind of your heart — *your subconscious mind.* It is the source of hunches, intuition, inspiration, and flashes of insight. It acts on impulse. It is also the seat of all your deep emotions: love, hate, anger, jealousy, and so on. *It does not think — it feels.*

"So remember these two ideas, George. *Your conscious mind thinks — your subconscious mind feels.* Sometimes they are in complete agreement with each other, but often they are not. And when reason and imagination are in conflict, imagination always wins. *The head never hears 'til the heart has listened.*

"To accomplish successfully whatever you set out to do, your conscious mind and your subconscious mind must be in full agreement with each other. You must convince your subconscious mind that the objective to be reached is really worth the effort to be expended. And you don't sell the subconscious mind on anything with facts and figures. It doesn't use or understand logic and reasoning.

"Let me give you a for-instance, George. You smoke even though you know cigarettes can cause lung cancer. Your conscious mind knows you ought to stop, but you reject its advice. Your subconscious mind tells you, 'Go ahead and smoke. It's okay. Enjoy yourself. You won't get lung cancer. Tom Jones or Bill Smith might get it, but you won't. Don't worry about it. Smoke all you want to.'

"So you do. You listen to your subconscious mind instead of your conscious mind. You do what you *feel* like doing or what you *want* to do, not what you know you ought to do.

"Or take another quick example, George. Statistics show that one out of every 13 people who drink becomes an alcoholic. But does that worry you? Does that keep you from taking a drink? Of course not.

"Your subconscious mind says, 'Go ahead and drink. You're not an alcoholic; you never could be. Might happen to the other fellow, but it won't happen to you. Drink up; dry the cup!'

"So you go right ahead and drink, don't you? Again, you listen to your subconscious mind instead of your conscious mind. You do what you *feel* like doing or what you *want* to do, no matter what the consequences might be.

"That's the same kind of situation you have here with your excess fat problem, George. I could give you a dozen good reasons why you ought to get rid of your extra pounds, but you wouldn't listen to me. Oh, you'd listen with your conscious mind and you'd even agree with me on the surface, but I wouldn't be able to reach your subconscious mind with logic and reasoning.

"And until your subconscious mind is convinced, unless it really feels you ought to reduce, your conscious mind alone will never get the job done for you, for *the head never hears 'til the heart has listened."*

George got my message loud and clear. He used my non-glue-food diet and meal-planning guide to go from 205 down to 165. His head finally heard when he listened to what I said with his heart.

How to find the real reason
you want to get rid of your excess fat

Now I want you to probe deep into your own subconscious

mind — your emotional mind, the mind of your heart — to find the *real* reason you want to reduce and get rid of your excess fat.

You see, most of us have two reasons for doing anything: one that sounds good to other people, and even to ourselves — that's the *ought-to reason;* and the real one, or the *want-to reason.*

When you reduce, you'll give your friends an ought-to reason. You'll tell them it was "doctor's orders. . .my high blood pressure. . .ticker was giving me trouble. . .stomach was out of whack. . .doctor said I might get diabetes. . ."

These ought-to reasons sound good, both to you and your friends, and of course they are good, sound, legitimate reasons that serve to justify your actions.

But the real reason you finally decided to reduce was. . .

You were sick and tired of people making fun of you; your husband had stopped paying attention to you; he wanted to get twin beds; had even stepped out on you; your son said you could get a job as the fat lady at the carnival; the sales girl actually laughed at you when you wanted to try on a size 14; maybe you felt just like one of my patients did when he told me, "Doc, I'm just sick and tired of being sick and tired!"

At any rate, these are just a few of the real want-to reasons fat people finally decide to reduce and get rid of their excess fat. And when you figure out your own real reason for wanting to lose your fat, and when you admit that reason to yourself so you'll actually understand why you're doing it, you'll be well on your way to a slim, trim, and youthful figure.

For instance, do you want to gain a greater measure of love from your husband? Do you want him to pay more attention to you, to appreciate you? Do you want to trim down so you can capture that new fellow who came to work in your office last week? Or could it be that your complexion is embarrassing you and you want to clear it up? It is a matter of pride, self-respect, self-esteem? Do you simply want to be more acceptable to yourself? Is that what's bothering you?

Any one or all of these reasons will work for you because they appeal to your heart — not your head; to your subconscious mind — not your conscious mind. So you must know *why* you really want to lose your excess fat before you can do so. Once you understand the deep emotional or subconscious reason you want to reduce, you'll be able to concentrate on that so you can get the job done.

You'll gain the motivation you need to get rid of your extra pounds. For unless your desire to reduce is great, your chances for success are much slimmer than you will ever be.

How to stimulate your subconscious mind to work for you

Remember that the first step in working with your subconscious mind is to bring the real reason for wanting to reduce into your conscious mind so you can fully understand it yourself.

Let's say you've already done that and your real reason for wanting to get rid of your excess fat is to be more attractive so you can win respect and admiration from your friends and acquaintances as well as more attention from a certain handsome young man. How do you then stimulate your subconscious mind to go to work for you so you can achieve this goal of yours? Here's how:

Start by seeing yourself in your mind's eye as being slim and trim. See yourself standing in front of your mirror without any clothes on. Picture yourself as being extremely attractive and desirable to your man. Imagine your face without all those extra layers of fat, your chin single — not double or triple. See your countenance as being interesting, beautiful, alive and glowing with vitality. Think of your body as being firm and trim, your arms slender and graceful, your waist without all those unsightly bulges, your hips sexy and seductive, your legs slim and shapely.

Next visualize yourself dressed in the latest fashion that will become you. No more droopy dresses, baggy blouses, or sagging skirts, but modern, up-to-date, well-fitted, stylish clothes.

Now imagine what your friends will say, how the men will

look at you, how their wives will be jealous of you, the offers that will come your way. Go ahead, enjoy yourself. Let yourself go. Wallow in those imaginary compliments.

Dream. . .pretend. . .imagine; let your ego get its fill. Sure, that's daydreaming. But *you are actually making promises to your subconscious mind* — your emotional mind, the mind of your heart. Your subconscious mind is also your storehouse of memory, so it will remember your promises and help you keep them.

Do everything you can right here, before going on, to convince your subconscious mind that losing your excess fat is really worthwhile. Just remember this maxim: *When your subconscious mind knows what your conscious mind really wants — you can always have it.*

"Doctor, how much should I really weigh?"

I always let my patients answer this question first for themselves. I'll ask you the same thing: How much do you think you really ought to weigh? Chances are, your answer will be far too high.

Some of the reasons for your high estimate are understandable. They could easily be carryovers from your childhood. Maybe your mother thought the best way she could show her love for you was to stuff you full of rich and sweet "glue-foods" such as her homemade pie, cake, and cookies. I'm sure your grandmother treated you the same way when you went over to her house. I know mine always did.

When you were fat and full, they were happy and contented. But if you happened to be a skinny child, everybody worried about you. They were so afraid you were undernourished — that you just weren't getting enough to eat. So they tried to force-feed you.

It could also be that you grew up in a family where cleaning up your plate was worthy of praise. If you ate everything your mother put on your plate for you to eat, you were a good boy. But if you didn't, you were a bad boy.

Of course, your father probably got into the act, too, for to him cleaning up your plate was a simple matter of economics as it is to any father who pays the bills.

Life insurance companies put out the most reliable weight charts, for they compile statistics for your best weight by actuarial life and death figures. They are vitally interested in keeping their policyholders alive, so they are naturally interested in determining the best weights for them.

In my office I use a large life insurance company's weight chart to help my fat patients determine their most desirable weight for their particular kind of frame. When you look at the following chart, you'll probably think the figures are far too low for you. My patients always do. But remember you have not yet learned to think of yourself as a slim person. You do not now realize how attractive you will become when you are actually trimmed down to your ideal weight.

How to establish a reasonable
and attainable weight goal

The best way to do this is to set some intermediate goals for yourself first. For instance, let's say you're a woman over 25 and you're 5'4" tall. If you happen to have a large frame, you could weigh from a top of 138 pounds down to 121; a medium frame, from 126 down to 113; a small frame, from 116 down to 108. Now that's a big range of weight allowance, actually from 138 pounds down to 108, or a difference of 30 pounds.

If you really do have a heavy or medium frame, you won't have to lose as much as if you had a small frame. But to tell the truth, you won't honestly know what kind of frame you actually do have until you've lost some of your excess fat.

In the beginning, I know you'll think you have a heavy frame — all my fat patients always think they do — for it will allow you to carry more weight. But after you reach the weight that's given for a heavy frame, you'll be surprised to find out you might not have a heavy frame after all. Only your excess fat made it seem that way to you.

Desirable Weights According to Frame
At Ages 25 and Over

Height With Shoes	Weight in Pounds in Indoor Clothing		
	Small Frame	Medium Frame	Large Frame
MEN 5′ 2″	112-120	118-129	126-141
4″	118-126	124-136	132-148
6″	124-133	130-143	138-156
8″	132-141	138-152	147-166
10″	140-150	146-160	155-174
6′ 0″	148-158	154-170	164-184
2″	156-167	162-180	173-194
4″	164-175	172-190	182-204
WOMEN 5′ 0″	96-104	101-113	109-125
2″	102-110	107-119	115-131
4″	108-116	113-126	121-138
6″	114-123	120-135	129-146
8″	122-131	128-143	137-154
10″	130-140	136-151	145-163
6′ 0″	138-148	144-159	153-173

*Courtesy of the Metropolitan Life Insurance Company.

If that's true in your case — and with 95 out of every 100 of my fat patients it is — then readjust your final goal, set some new intermediate goals, and keep right on going. Never allow yourself to stop short of your final goal. Don't mistake the beginning of your achievement for your final objective. Don't be satisfied with only partial success.

You will not need to worry about getting too thin or starving yourself to death on my non-glue-food diet. Your body will not let that happen to you. The non-glue-food diet is not a starvation diet, nor is it a crash diet. You'll be able to eat as much as you want even while you're losing as much as you want. When you reach your most desirable weight from your body's innate point of view, you'll not lose any more. You'll stabilize there.

How to use inches instead of pounds as your goal

"Doctor, I want to lose ten pounds," a patient once said to me.

But when she got on the scales, I saw that she should actually lose closer to 50 pounds. Did I tell her that? Of course not. Had I done so then, I would have totally destroyed her desire to lose even ten pounds. So instead I said, "Yes, Anna, you're right. You really should lose at least ten pounds, perhaps even a little bit more."

"How much more do I have to lose, Doctor?" she asked, a dismal and discouraged look on her face.

"Well, let's not worry about that right now, Anna," I said, knowing that whatever answer I gave would completely kill any desire she had to reduce. "Instead of thinking about how many pounds you should lose, let's go at it from a different angle, shall we? For instance, *why don't you go for just one dress size smaller,* Anna? After you reach that goal, then we'll reassess the situation and see what more needs to be done."

That's how Anna reduced. She got rid of her excess baggage on my non-glue-food diet — not by counting the pounds she had to lose — but by measuring her excess fat loss in smaller dress sizes.

If my patient is a man who's scared to think in pounds of excess fat, I talk to him in terms of tightening the belt a couple of inches — going from a 44 waist down to a 42, "and then we'll see what we ought to do after that."

An effective technique for losing fat

Whether you take off pounds or inches, the results will all be the same. You're getting rid of your excess fat and that's what really counts. All I'm interested in doing is helping my fat patients find the right psychological handle to grab hold of. This is one time when any means you can use to reach the end you want is completely justified.

If you can't think in pounds of fat, then your best bet is always to think in inches of circumference. Always go for the next smaller size. Work your way down, size by size, until the scales no longer frighten you. Then you can check your weight by your height and frame.

However, if you can think in pounds of fat instead of inches of circumference from the beginning, then start with your height, be as honest as you can about your frame, and when you reach the top end of your weight range, aim for the low end of it. After you've held that new weight for a couple of months or so, you'll become used to seeing yourself as a slim person. Then you'll be better able to determine whether you've misjudged your frame or not.

Either way will work easily for you, for no effort is required on the non-glue-food diet to get rid of your excess fat. In fact, the non-glue-food diet is so easy you don't have to work at it; you just let it work for you.

You don't need to count calories, weigh or measure your food; you don't have to memorize anything. In fact, you won't even need to use willpower to reduce on the non-glue-food diet, as you'll see right now.

You don't need willpower to get rid
of your excess fat

Does this seem like a different idea to you? Most diets you've tried before always demanded that you use your willpower, right? And you always failed, true?

Well, this time it's going to be different. This time you don't need willpower to get rid of your excess fat. In fact, I'd rather you didn't use willpower at all. It's a hindrance, not a help.

Controlling a problem always takes willpower

You see, it always takes willpower to *control* a problem; but you can never use willpower to *solve* it. For instance, I've never known anyone in all my life (and that includes me, too) who could ever solve a single solitary personal problem and *keep it solved* by using willpower. Oh, you might push your problem aside temporarily by using willpower, but it'll always be there, waiting to come back to you whenever your willpower fades out, as it always will. You'll never solve any personal problem by resisting it, by fighting it, or by trying to control it with willpower. You'll always end up doing what you want to do — if you really want to do it badly enough — and willpower be damned! Whenever reason (willpower) and imagination (desire) are in conflict, imagination will win. The head never hears 'til the heart has listened. Remember?

Not fighting your problem, not resisting it, not trying to control it is the only real solution. The only answer that ever really works to solve any personal problem — whether it's drinking, smoking, gambling, or overeating — is not to use your willpower to control that problem, but to turn your back on it, walk away from it, put it out of your mind, and forget it completely.

How the no-willpower concept works

Let's take an alcoholic, for example. "An alcoholic wants to learn how to solve his problem of alcoholism by controlling the amount he drinks," Carl S. says. "But he never will solve his drinking problem that way for the alcoholic doesn't live who can take just one drink and quit. It is absolutely impossible for him to control his alcoholism by using willpower to space his drinks.

"The only way the alcoholic can ever solve his drinking problem is not to use willpower to control how much he drinks, but to turn his back on the bottle, walk away from it, put it out of his mind, and forget it completely."

Quitting smoking works exactly the same way. Most people try to quit by cutting down first. They try to use willpower to control the number of cigarettes they smoke each day; but they always fail. If you're trying to quit by slowing down or by controlling the number of cigarettes you smoke each day, quit kidding yourself. You might be able to control your cigarette consumption for awhile by smoking one every hour on the hour. But then along comes a crisis and all your good intentions go down the drain as you light up one cigarette after another in a vain attempt to calm your nerves.

The only way you can ever stop smoking and make it stick is to do exactly as the alcoholic does. Don't use willpower to control the number of cigarettes you smoke each day, but simply turn your back on your smoking problem, walk away from cigarettes, and completely forget them. That is the only way you'll ever be able to solve your problem. I know; I've been there. That's the only method that works.

Here's how this technique applies to losing excess fat

Now that I've given you a couple of examples to show you that willpower does not work in solving your personal problems, let's take a look at your own specific trouble: your excess fat.

What's the solution to your problem? The same as before. The answer is not to use your willpower in a vain attempt to control the amount of rich and fattening glue-foods that you eat. *The answer is not to eat any of the glue-foods that make you fat.* Don't try to use willpower to control your glue-food intake by eating just a little bit of them. Don't allow yourself even one little bite; that's the one that causes all your trouble.

"I know this technique works," my patient Carl says. "I used it to stop drinking and I used it again to stop eating the glue-foods that made me so fat. Sticking to your non-glue-food diet was easy for me, Doc, just as long as I didn't try to use willpower to control the amount of glue-foods I ate. The answer for me was to handle glue-foods just as I handled alcohol: complete abstinence. I turned my back on them completely and didn't eat them at all. I didn't allow myself even one little bite.

"Glue-foods are just like alcohol. Once you start eating them, you can't stop. In AA we say it isn't the tenth or eleventh drink that gets you drunk — it's the first one. Eating glue-foods is exactly the same if you're a *foodaholic.* It isn't the tenth or eleventh bite that gets you fat — it's the first one!"

Here's how to forget your excess fat problem so you can solve it

The best way to forget your excess fat problem so you can solve it is to *concentrate on its solution.* If you continue to think about your problem you will keep right on resisting it and fighting to control it.

For instance, if an alcoholic gets sober on the AA program but continues to dream about the good old days when he could drink, he's headed for trouble again. Or if you stop smoking but constantly imagine how good a cigarette would taste with your morning coffee or after an evening meal, you'll some day start smoking again unless you learn to take your mind completely off your problem.

To get your mind off your own problem of excess fat, don't think about all those rich and fattening glue-foods you want to eat. Instead, concentrate on all those benefits that will be yours when you're slim and trim.

Irene's experience

One of my patients, Irene R., continued to fight the problem of getting rid of her excess fat. She wanted to prove to herself that she had the willpower to resist her desire for sweets, so she put a box of cherry chocolates on the dining table and then sat down to stare glumly at them, vowing to herself not to touch a single one.

The final outcome? She ate the entire box of candy, of course. What else could she do? Under such circumstances, she really had no other choice.

But today she's thin. She's no longer carrying around her excess fat. She got rid of it on my non-glue-food diet. However, before she was able to do that, she had to learn how *not* to use her willpower.

When you fight your problem the way Irene did — when you antagonize any unfavorable situation — you simply give it more power over you. You deplete your own power to gain victory to that same extent. Many times, especially at first glance, resistance seems to be the only way out. It seems to be the only way to get rid of those undesirable things that are bothering you. Unfortunately, bombarding your problem with willpower could easily cause you to be stuck with it. The opposite course — nonresistance — is the only way out.

When you offer mental nonresistance, your problem will crumble away and disappear right before your eyes. Many times, no further action will be needed from you than just that one thing — nonresistance.

Why you're going to succeed this time

So many fat people lose hundreds of pounds over and over again. They put a lot of effort into their diet attempts, yet they always fail. If you've done all this before yourself, then you know that's a great deal of hard work for nothing. It really takes a lot more effort to fail than it does to succeed.

But this time you're going to succeed. I don't care how many times you've failed before — this time you're going to make it. How can I be so sure of that? Because I've seen hundreds of others do the same by following my simple non-glue-food diet.

I'm sure you've tried many other diet plans and failed to reduce and get rid of your excess fat. Who hasn't? But don't worry about that now. The diet failures you had in the past are exactly that: failures. Leave them in the past where they belong. Let them stay buried. Forget them. They have nothing at all to do with the present. *Know that this time you're going to succeed.*

2. How the non-glue-food diet works when other diets fail

The reason the non-glue-food diet will work for you when all your other diet attempts have failed in the past is extremely simple:

The non-glue-food diet eliminates the cause of your excess fat. All those other diets you tried before did not.

When you eliminate the basic cause of your excess fat, when you get rid of the source of your problem, when you stop supplying the fuel that puts on those extra pounds, you'll benefit by losing your excess fat quickly, safely, easily, and permanently.

SECTION I. Why the Low-Calorie Diet Does Not Work For Permanent Weight Loss

The reason the low-calorie diet does not work is that it is based on an incorrect theory. Let me explain this now in detail.

The low-calorie concept is this: to lose weight, you must cut down on the number of calories you consume. The traditional management of obesity by most doctors has been based on the first law of thermodynamics: *energy can neither be created nor destroyed.* In other words, if your energy input in the form of food and drink is greater than your energy output in the form of exercise, heat production, and body metabolism, you will gain weight. If the reverse is true, that is to say if your expenditure of energy is greater than your input of food and drink, you will lose weight. That, in a nutshell, is the low-calorie theory.

This theory sounds good and it has led many doctors to devise all sorts of low-calorie diets, most of which reduce food input almost to the starvation level. Yet 95 percent of the time such diets are completely useless and ineffective. The dieter simply does not get rid of his excess fat, and here's why:

This law of thermodynamics applies to human physiology, too

Now if the law of the conservation of energy applies to human physiology just as it does to thermodynamics (and it most certainly does) then *reducing your energy input by cutting down the number of calories you take in will also lower your energy output or your ability to do work.*

Cutting down on your caloric intake or your energy input (which reduces your energy output or your ability to do work) does not necessarily mean that you will automatically burn up excess fat. It only means that you will have less energy available to perform your daily tasks. Remember: energy is neither created nor destroyed. That's the first law of thermodynamics.

The low-calorie diet and that tired feeling

For example, George Bray at the Tufts University School of Medicine found that people on low-calorie diets did not necessarily get rid of their excess fat just by taking in fewer calories than they normally did. He did find, however, that *they had far less energy available to burn.*

I've found the same thing to be true, too, for I've had patient after patient tell me, "Doctor, I was so exhausted and worn out when I went on a low-calorie diet I was afraid to try your non-glue-food diet because I simply didn't want to go through that miserable process all over again.

"But your non-glue-food diet is so different. I get all I want to eat and I'm not tired and nervous and worn out as I was when I dieted before. I can zip through my housework now where I used to drag around all day and still not get it done. And the wonderful part of your diet is that I'm actually losing weight and feeling good all at the same time."

If you've ever agonized through a low-calorie diet before, you too know that you have less energy to do your daily work. You are constantly tired and worn out. Your nerves, your personality, your productivity all suffer. You run the very real risk of losing your husband, your wife, your friends, even your job.

The low-calorie diet and muscle-tissue loss

Not only that, if you do happen to lose some weight on a low-calorie diet, chances are you'll lose far more vital muscle tissue than fat. This has been proved by scientifically controlled experiments in low-calorie diets at the Oak Knoll Hospital in Oakland, California, and at the Georgetown University School of Medicine in Washington, D. C.

For instance, at the Oak Knoll Hospital, the doctors determined that fat tissue accounted for only 35 percent of weight loss while vital muscle tissue accounted for 65 percent in low-calorie diets. The studies conducted at the Georgetown University School of Medicine confirmed the Oak Knoll Hospital findings that *twice as much lean muscle tissue as fat is lost on low-calorie diets.* Lawrence Kyle and Michael Ball discovered that on low-calorie diets, 66 percent of the weight loss was vital muscle tissue while only 34 percent was fat.

The slight difference of one percent (65 to 66 and 35 to 34) resulted from different methods of analysis of weight loss. However, these studies do confirm conclusively that a low-calorie diet is neither an effective nor an efficient way to get rid of excess fat.

In fact, the loss of such vital body tissue other than fat on a low-calorie diet will soon lead to a run-down and worn-out physical condition. Not only that, you can also see from these experiments that on a low-calorie diet you will often lose weight in the wrong places when you lose muscle tissue instead of fat. One of my patients, Sandra, was a victim of this syndrome before she came to me.

"Each time I tried to diet before, I ended up looking like a scarecrow," Sandra told me. "I was losing more muscle tissue than fat tissue. My arms got thinner and I felt weaker. I had no strength any more in my legs. My face got thin and haggard-looking, but I still had my double chin and my fat stomach.

"Your non-glue-food diet changed things completely for me, Doctor. I was able to lose fat − not just weight − and I got rid of it in the right places this time. Not only that, your meal-planning guide with its excellent food values kept my energy high at all times. I never felt worn out, exhausted, and drained of energy as I did when I was on a low-calorie diet."

The low-calorie diet and regained weight

Since you cannot stay on the low-calorie diet indefinitely without depleting your vitality, lowering your resistance to infection, courting anemia, or eventually ruining your health completely, you have to stop dieting sometime. When you do, you will inevitably gain back whatever weight you've lost, and usually more besides.

But in spite of all this, most people have used the low-calorie diet for weight control for years simply because they've known of nothing better.

The failure of the low-calorie diet to help fat people reduce successfully has led to any number of fad diets: the grapefruit diet; the soup diet; the melon and cottage cheese diet; the grapefruit and steak diet; and many others. In fact, any new diet that promises to reduce a person's weight is often said to be the answer to the circulation problems of many a failing magazine.

To wrap up the low-calorie diet in a neat little package so we can throw it away and be done with it once and for all, let me simply say that *it does not work because our bodies do not treat all food calories the same way.* Proteins, carbohydrates, and fats all act differently in the body, as you'll see later on in this chapter when I discuss their functions in complete detail.

SECTION II: What You've Always Wanted to Know About Foods Causing Overweight

I became interested in the problem of obesity shortly after I went into my chiropractic practice because of my inability to give any sort of lasting relief to my fat patients who suffered from nagging low backache. I knew they needed to reduce before I could do anything permanent about their backache. However, I was in no position to advise any of my patients how to get rid of their excess fat, for I was 45 pounds overweight myself. I simply could not offer them any sort of diet that would be even half-way successful.

In fact, had I known of any diet that really worked to take off excess fat, I would have used it myself, for I'd tried all kinds of diets with absolutely no results: low-calorie diets; grapefruit; cottage cheese; and various other fad diets, crash diets and starvation diets. Nothing ever seemed to work for me. I'd lose five to ten pounds — 15 at the most — but I would always gain it right back every time just as soon as I stopped dieting.

Each time I tried to lose weight, I became unfit to live with. I was nervous, irritable, jumpy, out-of-sorts, and I couldn't sleep. When you deal with the public every day as I do, you can't afford to go around with an attitude like that. So I finally gave up dieting altogether. I decided I was just meant to be fat — period.

How my term "glue-foods" evolved

One day one of my fat patients said to me, "Doc, I think our trouble is everything we eat seems to be made out of glue. We must be eating *glue-foods* because they sure seem to stick to us!"

"I believe you're right, Alice," I said. "At least, it sure seems that way."

"I tell you what, Doc," she said. "If *glue-foods* make us fat, maybe you can come up with a list of *non-glue-foods* that wouldn't stick to us so we could get thin. If you ever do find a diet like that, be sure and let me know; I'd really like to try it."

I mentioned this conversation to my wife that night and we both laughed about it. "I wish it were that simple," I said. "I wish there were such things as *glue-foods* and *non-glue-foods*. It would sure solve a lot of problems for fat people like Alice and me."

My wife looked thoughtful for a moment and then she said, "Could be that *glue-food* is the clue you've been looking for all along. Remember how we used to make glue out of flour and water when we were kids? Maybe all the foods that have flour in them really are glue-foods so they actually do stick to you. Maybe that's why you're overweight."

Glue-food is the real reason people get fat

Well, my wife was right. Glue-food is the culprit for sure; it is wholly at fault. *Eating too much glue-food is the real reason people get so fat.*

Of course, the bio-chemistry of excess fat production is quite complicated, and food doesn't actually turn into glue in your body, but it sure seems as if it does for it really does stick to you like glue.

But at least Alice's remarks and my wife's comments got me on the right track, so I was finally able to solve the problem of excess fat for myself and my fat patients.

The author's experience

Now I had to experiment on myself first so I could prove or disprove this idea, so I made up a list of glue-foods to avoid. I jotted down all the ones I could think of with flour in them: cake; pie; cookies; rolls; doughnuts; pastries of all sorts; bread; cereals; pancakes; waffles; french toast; spaghetti; macaroni; noodles; and so on. I started my own "non-glue-food" diet just by avoiding these foods. But other than not eating those foods with flour in them, I set no restrictions of any sort on what I ate. By the end of the first month, I'd lost 12 pounds by not eating the glue-foods that contained flour, and I hadn't starved myself at all. I hadn't been ravenously hungry all the time as I'd always been when I'd dieted before.

I continued to eat this way, and before the year was over, 33 more pounds of excess fat had melted away. I went from 192 down to 147 for a total loss of 45 pounds and there I've stayed ever since without any trouble at all.

Alice saw the physical changes that were taking place in me and she wanted to know what was going on. When I told her, she insisted that she be allowed to experiment right along with me, especially when she learned how her remarks had given me the whole idea of glue-foods and non-glue-foods in the first place. So she was really my first patient to use my non-glue-food diet. And the diet worked for her, too. She went from 218 pounds down to 135 in that first year for a total loss of 83 pounds.

Of course, during that year I made some additional changes and I added a few refinements to my original non-glue-food diet. For instance, I soon realized that most foods with flour in them also had sugar, so I eliminated all granulated refined sugar from my diet as well as any foods that contained it. And getting rid of foods with flour in them automatically got rid of cornstarch, another glue-food. Still others — ice cream and fruit canned in syrup, for example — were added to my list as I went along. I'll discuss some more of the ones I added when I take up my non-glue-food diet in complete detail in Chapter 3.

Glue-food consumption is the major
cause of overweight

At least 95 out of every 100 fat people eat too much glue-food. That's the sole reason they are so fat. No more than five, probably even less, out of every 100 can actually blame their excess fat on glandular disturbances.

Even those with glandular problems still eat far too much glue-food; thus, only part of their excess fat can be blamed on their glands. The rest of it comes from eating too much glue-food.

Since glue-foods cause your excess fat, too, you'll need to take two definite concrete steps to eliminate that cause.

1. You must stop eating glue-foods so you can cut off the source of supply of your excess fat.
2. You must take positive action to burn up the excess fat that has accumulated in your body from eating too much glue-food over the years.

As I'm sure you realize by now, glue-food is a coined term of mine. You'll not find it in the dictionary. I use it because it is so descriptive of certain foods that act like glue and stick to your body just like glue in the form of fat when you eat them.

When you eat a *non-glue-food* — which is also a coined phrase of mine — you encounter no such problem, for it is digested, metabolized, and then passed on through your body as a waste product after performing its necessary and vital functions without causing any buildup of excess fat.

But a glue-food literally acts like glue in your body. It piles up layer upon layer and you can't get rid of it. It sticks to you long after you've eaten it and causes problems of overweight that are difficult to solve.

Glue-foods are actually man-made carbohydrate foods

Glue-foods are foods that contain *sugar, flour,* or *starch* that has been *added, increased,* or *changed* in some way during the manufacturing process. These man-made sources of carbohydrates include, but are not necessarily limited to: refined sugar; flour; starch; such compound foods as cereals, soft drinks, candy; ice cream; puddings; desserts of all kinds; bakery products such as bread, rolls, doughnuts; pastries of all sorts; pie; cookies; cake; pasta such as spaghetti, macaroni, and noodles.

Glue foods also include dried fruits — for example, raisins and prunes — since the sugar content has been increased in comparison to the weight during the dehydration process. A pound of raisins has much more sugar than a pound of grapes, for instance. The increased sugar content comes from the loss of water.

Some canned goods are glue-foods; others are not. For example, fruit canned in its natural state or just with water added is not a glue-food. But when refined sugar or syrup is added to sweeten it, then it becomes a glue-food.

If you find yourself in a quandry as to whether a food is or is not a glue-food that should be avoided, learn to read the label thoroughly. The labels on all canned or packaged compound foods must show all the ingredients used in the manufacturing process. If you see the words *sugar, dextrose, flour,* or *starch,* then you know without doubt that it's a glue-food.

The test for glue-food

If there's no label to read that shows the ingredients — for example, raisins or prunes — just ask yourself this one simple question: *was any sugar, flour, or starch added, increased, or changed in any way during the manufacturing process?* If your answer is "Yes," then it's a glue-food and it will make you fat. Don't eat it. If your answer is "No," then it's a non-glue-food. Go ahead and eat it. It will keep you slim, trim, and healthy.

"The non-glue-food diet is the easiest diet to follow I've ever seen," Barry told me. "It's so simple and easy to understand. All you need do is remember not to eat any of the glue-foods that contain sugar, flour, or starch. How much simpler can a diet get than that?

"And the most wonderful thing of all about it is that it really works. The results are fantastic. Take me for instance, Doc. I think I'd tried every diet under the sun and failed to lose weight. But on the non-glue-food diet I went from 232 down to 175 for a loss of 57 pounds in less than a year. How can you beat that?"

How glue-foods work to make you fat

Glue-foods, or man-made carbohydrates, contain very little if any bulk, such as the cellulose and fiber found in the natural sources of carbohydrates such as fruit and vegetables. Most glue-foods are man-made carbohydrates in the form of sugar, flour, or starch. A glue-food does not contain any, or at least very little protein, fat or natural carbohydrates. You can stuff yourself with them all day long and never really be satisfied for any great length of time because sugar and starch digest so quickly. They are absorbed almost immediately into your bloodstream. Your stomach becomes physically empty soon after eating a glue-food, and almost immediately, you're hungry again.

To fully understand why glue-foods cause your excess fat, you need to know just a little bit more about the way carbohydrates are used in your body.

Your body uses carbohydrates as a source of energy

Carbohydrates are used by your body as a source of energy. However, when you eat more man-made carbohydrates (glue-foods) than you need for *immediate* energy requirements, the surplus is always changed into fat and stored in your body for future use. Unfortunately, from the standpoint of both health and appearance, the amount of man-made carbohydrate (glue-food) that can be converted into permanent body fat and stored by your body is virtually unlimited.

Here's a specific example of how glue-foods make you fat

"Why do glue-foods make me so fat, Doc?" a fat patient asked me as we sat in my consultation room talking about his excess fat problem.

"I can best explain that to you by discussing your normal food intake, Sam," I said. "You've already told me that you're trying to cut down on what you eat because you want to reduce. Trouble is, you're going about it the wrong way.

"For instance, you told me that you're skipping breakfast. That won't help you lose weight, Sam, for when you don't eat enough or when you miss a meal, your blood sugar falls, causing symptoms you already know only too well.

"You become tense, irritable, and overly tired. You get a headache. You feel miserable all over and your body develops an insatiable craving for something sweet.

"Well, if you're like most fat people, Sam, and I know from our conversation that you are, you'll go on a *sweet binge.* You'll overeat at the next meal or you'll probably stuff yourself even before then at your mid-morning coffee break with such glue-foods as doughnuts, sweet rolls, pastry, pie, cake, or some other sweet dessert.

"When you do that, your body will absorb more sugar into the bloodstream than it needs to meet your immediate energy requirements. Your blood sugar rises above normal limits and your body reacts at once to get rid of your hyperglycemia.

"Your pancreas is stimulated to produce insulin so the excess sugar in your blood can be converted into permanent body fat. Otherwise, the excess sugar in your blood will spill over into your urine as it does in diabetes.

"You see, a fat person's pancreas actually becomes 'trigger-happy' because of the constant input of sugar into his bloodstream from the glue-foods he's always eating. A fat person always develops low blood sugar and intense hunger pangs much sooner than a thin person does because his pancreas actually becomes overefficient.

"When the excess sugar in your blood is converted into

permanent body fat because you don't need it for immediate energy, your blood sugar again falls below normal limits. Again, you experience symptoms of hypoglycemia: tension; irritability; headache; excessive fatigue; nausea; and an insatiable craving for sweets.

"What do you do then, Sam? Well, if it's time for lunch, you'll probably load yourself down with glue-foods again: bread; rolls; spaghetti; pizza; cake; pie alamode; etc. You leave no room at all for high-energy non-glue-foods. Or if it's mid-afternoon, you'll grab a couple of doughnuts or a sweet roll, maybe a piece of cake, with your coffee break. You might even take a candy bar or two back to your desk. And that same vicious cycle repeats itself.

"More sugar is absorbed into your bloodstream than can be used at once by your body for immediate energy. Your pancreas produces insulin to convert the excess blood sugar into permanent body fat so it won't spill over into the urine. Your blood sugar falls, and there you are; right back in the same old rut. The unfortunate part of all this is, *the more glue-foods you eat — the hungrier and fatter you become.*

"You go home from the office each day absolutely exhausted whether you did or didn't get any work done, and you can't understand why you feel so tired and worn out all the time. Your natural tendency is to blame the way you feel on the fast pace of earning a living or the intense pressure of these modern times you live in, when to tell the truth, Sam, if you'd just stop eating those glue-foods, you'd feel like a million every day. You'd have all the energy your body needed to burn and you wouldn't get fat either."

What's the answer to your own excess fat problem? Well, I can tell you the same thing I told Sam: Stop eating those glue-foods that make you fat. Start eating the non-glue-foods that make you slim and trim. When you do that, you'll find you can get rid of your excess fat just as quickly and easily as Sam did. He went from 240 down to 180 in seven months by avoiding glue-foods and by following my non-glue-food diet and my meal-planning guide. You can do the same, for it's as simple and easy as that.

Most fat people are foodaholics

Almost all fat people are *foodaholics*. Because of their damaged carbohydrate metabolism, they are no longer able to control their intake of glue-foods. They have a craving, a compulsion, an obsession to eat man-made carbohydrates just as an alcoholic has a craving, a compulsion, an obsession to drink liquor.

Carl S. tells me that an alcoholic can no longer control his drinking, but that his drinking controls him. If he could control his intake of alcohol, he wouldn't be an alcoholic.

The same thing can be said about a foodaholic. A foodaholic can no longer control his intake of glue-foods; instead, glue-foods control him. If he could control his intake of glue-foods, he wouldn't be fat; he wouldn't be a foodaholic.

As long as an alcoholic doesn't take the first drink, he is not troubled with his drinking problem. But the moment he does, his obsession for alcohol becomes overpowering and it is impossible for him to stop drinking.

A foodaholic is the same. As long as he doesn't take the first bite of a glue-food, he's okay. But the moment he does, his craving for sweet glue-foods overpowers him and he is unable to control his desire for them.

Adena's experience

"As long as I don't take the first bite of pie or cake or ice cream, I'm all right," Adena told me. "But the moment I do, then I can't stop eating until I'm completely stuffed.

"Why, before I went on your non-glue-food diet, Doctor, I used to make a chocolate cake and sit down and eat the whole thing all by myself. But I no longer have that craving for glue-foods I used to have. I'm completely satisfied and full with the foods I eat on your non-glue-food diet. Besides, I don't want that extra 50 pounds back to drag around. I'm happy with things just the way they are right now. I wouldn't trade my 122 pounds for a piece of chocolate cake or pie alamode any day of the week!"

Don't get the wrong idea of what a foodaholic is. There's nothing moral or immoral about being a foodaholic. To be a foodaholic is not a sin. A foodaholic has a disease — the disease of abnormal carbohydrate metabolism.

Review your own normal daily food intake

I know you think you're not a foodaholic, and maybe you're not. But before you make up your mind for sure, let me ask you this: Have you ever finished a big meal and almost immediately afterward had a terrific craving for candy or something sweet? If you have, chances are you're a foodaholic, for such an untimely hunger craving for something sweet even when you're physically full is a major sign of a damaged or abnormal carbohydrate metabolism.

The best way to determine whether you're a foodaholic or not is simply to review your own regular daily food intake. You won't need a pencil and paper to do this. Just think about what you ate yesterday or the day before or what your regular daily eating habits actually are.

I will say that when you snack between meals, if you eat a piece of meat or cheese or some other high-protein food instead of pie or cake or cookies or candy, you're probably not a foodaholic. But if your daily food consumption is similar to Sam's, then the odds are that you're a foodaholic and the non-glue-food diet is just the thing for you.

Why don't glue-foods make everybody fat?

Glue-foods don't make everyone fat for the same reason that drinking liquor doesn't make everyone an alcoholic. By the same token, not all people are diabetics or cardiac cases either.

The fat person is allergic to glue-foods

The fat person is allergic to glue-foods just as a diabetic is allergic to sugar or an alcoholic is allergic to alcohol. An alcoholic's body can't tolerate alcohol; he can't drink without getting drunk. A diabetic's body can't tolerate sugar; he can't eat it without getting sick. A fat person's body can't tolerate glue-foods; he can't eat them without getting fat.

Now a great many people can eat bread, rolls, cookies, cake, macaroni, spaghetti, noodles, and other such foods all their lives and not get fat. That's wonderful; more power to them. To them, such substances are food. But to a fat person, they're poison.

You see, I'm not advocating that we should do away with all such foods for everyone. I'm simply saying that fat people should do away with them if they want to get rid of their excess fat so they can be healthy and happy.

Teenagers

I will say, however, that even thin people with skin problems — especially teenagers with acne — can benefit greatly by following the non-glue-food diet, too. In most cases, their skin conditions will clear up completely when they follow this diet and eat only non-glue-foods.

My office files are full of case histories of thin teenagers whose skin problems were completely solved by my non-glue-food diet. Let me tell you of just one instance.

Laura was an extremely attractive high school junior. She had only one problem: acne. Although she ate an excessive amount of glue-foods, as so many young people do, she was not troubled with a weight problem.

She learned about the non-glue-food diet from a classmate of hers who had used it successfully to get rid of 30 pounds. But the loss of weight didn't impress Laura; what impressed her was the improvement of her girlfriend's complexion.

So she came to see me. I placed her on the non-glue-food diet and within a few months her face had cleared up and her skin was beautiful. It was alive and glowing with radiant health. Laura is only one of many who have so benefited.

Why do people eat so many glue-foods?

There are a variety of reasons. However, I'll discuss briefly three of the most important ones: *economy; convenience; taste.*

Economy. Glue-foods are always cheaper than non-glue-foods. Man-made carbohydrates such as pancakes, bread, rolls, spaghetti, macaroni and noodles always cost much less than natural sources of carbohydrates such as fresh fruits and vegetables, fats such as butter and eggs, proteins such as meat, fish, poultry, and cheese.

Bread has always been called the poor-man's protein. The sources of man-made sugar, starch, and flour in the average diet are cheap and plentiful. For instance, if you eat cereal, rolls, or doughnuts for breakfast, it's a lot cheaper than ham, bacon, or steak and eggs.

Convenience. Glue-foods are easier to prepare than non-glue-foods. It's a lot quicker and simpler to send Johnny or Susie off to school on time with a bowl of dry cereal and a roll or a doughnut than to cook bacon and eggs. It saves you time in the morning and that's important to most people.

Glue-food snacks are also a lot more convenient to prepare than non-glue-food snacks. In fact, the manufacturer goes all out to make things extremely convenient for you. Take a look at the TV snack and tidbit counter in your grocery store next time you go shopping, and you'll see what I mean.

Taste. We all have a sweet tooth. Unfortunately, it's overdeveloped to the point where we will no longer accept good fresh fruit to satisfy our sweet tooth. We insist on cake, candy, pie, ice cream, and all sorts of empty sweets and rich desserts.

But this bad habit can be broken. You can still satisfy your sweet tooth by re-educating your taste buds to accept sweet non-glue-foods that are good for you instead of the sweet glue-foods that make you fat and ruin your teeth to boot.

Here's what happens in your body when you don't eat glue-foods

"Before I went on your non-glue-food diet, my average breakfast was two doughnuts and a cup of coffee," Glen told me. "By ten in the morning I was absolutely exhausted. I didn't think I could make it through the day. I was really worried, for I was only 36 years old.

"But then I went to bacon and eggs or ham and eggs for breakfast on your non-glue-food diet. What a difference, Doc. I'm not worn out any more at all. Your diet really put a tiger in my tank!"

One of the main reasons the non-glue-food diet will work so well for you is that when you stop eating glue-foods, you'll get rid of your hunger pangs and your constant desire to eat. You'll soon find out that proteins and fats satisfy you. But as you saw in Sam's case, when you eat man-made carbohydrates all the time, they actually make you hungry, for they stimulate the release of insulin, and that makes your blood sugar fall.

But on the non-glue-food diet your body metabolism will change so you can lose your excess fat without being hungry all the time. Here's what actually happens:

The pituitary hormone action

When you stop eating man-made carbohydrates, your body increases the production of a hormone from the pituitary gland that is used in the metabolism of fat. This pituitary hormone causes your body to shift from its usual metabolism of man-made carbohydrates over to the metabolism of fats to meet your energy requirements.

This hormone, which is secreted in abundance when there is no man-made carbohydrate in your diet, performs these four metabolic functions in your body that make you lose weight and help you to get rid of your excess fat:

1. It stops the deposition of any further body fat;
2. It uses the fat in your diet for your immediate energy

requirements;
3. It increases the utilization of your stored body fat to meet your current energy needs;
4. It decreases the carbohydrate requirements of your body by burning fat for energy instead.

You might think your body needs some man-made carbohydrates to burn for energy, but it does not. As you've just seen, when glue-foods are not present in your diet, your body burns fat for energy instead.

There are absolutely no harmful side effects from the non-glue-food diet. This has been proved scientifically many times in various diet experiments.

Let me quote Dr. Philip K. Bondy, Chairman of the Department of Internal Medicine at Yale University Medical School, who, in effect, says this: "No carbohydrate is necessary in the diet. It has been shown by experiments time and again that human beings can live in good health for month after month on a diet of meats and fats."

Now that you know that the man-made carbohydrates or the glue-foods are not needed in your diet for you to be healthy, and now that you also know they are the direct cause of your excess fat, let's leave them so we can move on to the next section in this chapter.

There you'll learn all about non-glue-foods and why they'll keep you slim, trim, healthy, and in tip-top shape.

SECTION III: How to Select Foods That Help You Lose Weight Without Regrets

Non-glue-foods are *proteins, fats,* and *natural sources of carbohydrates* such as fruits and vegetables. I'd like to discuss each one of these foods with you so you'll understand why they'll keep you slim, trim, healthy, and in tip-top shape.

Proteins are important non-glue-foods

The basic material of each one of your body cells is protein. Proteins are the main constituents, other than water, of the lean tissues of your body. A child needs protein daily for proper growth and development. An adult needs protein daily to replace and repair worn-out tissues. Protein is also used to heal wounds and to form scar tissue.

Animal proteins are of better nutritional value than plant proteins. However, a diet containing both animal and plant proteins is nutritionally and economically desirable. The best protein sources for you on the non-glue-food diet are eggs, cheese, fish and seafood, meats, poultry, and fresh vegetables.

Proteins are also used to build muscle tissue, blood, and bone. Your body never uses protein to meet its immediate energy requirements except in an emergency such as starvation. Nor does your body convert protein into fat for future energy use. You can see from this, then, that *you cannot possibly eat enough protein to get fat.*

Fats are also non-glue-foods

Strange as it might seem to you right now, *fats are not glue-foods.* The reason for this will become clear to you as we discuss the metabolism of fat in the body.

Excellent sources of fat for you on the non-glue-food diet will be natural fats in meats, canned fish and seafood, cheese, butter, margarine, edible oils, shortenings, most salad dressings, and egg yolks. On the non-glue-food diet, in sharp contrast to other diets, you can also use fats in your cooking to make your food more appetizing and palatable.

Fats are sources of energy. They are more than twice as "rich" as carbohydrates in calories per gram so they are really a more efficient body fuel than the glue-foods or the man-made carbohydrates.

When you do not eat enough man-made carbohydrates to meet your body's immediate energy requirements, your own body fat will be used instead. This helps you burn up some of your excess fat so you can get rid of it.

Fats, just like carbohydrates, can be used in only two ways by your body: to meet current energy needs, or to be stored as permanent fat for future energy requirements. Just like carbohydrates, fats cannot be used to build muscle tissue, blood, or bone.

Differences between fats and carbohydrates

Although fats and carbohydrates are both used for energy, here the similarity ends, for there is a tremendous difference in the way they are metabolized in the body.

When more carbohydrate is absorbed into your body than can be used for immediate energy, it must be converted into permanent body fat at once or be lost in the urine. But this is not true if there is excess fat in the bloodstream. The excess fat is *not* immediately changed into permanent body fat to be stored in your body as the excess man-made carbohydrates are. Instead, it is held in temporary storage in the liver and the lymphatic vessels until it is needed at a later time in the body for energy. Then it is sent to that part of the body where it is needed.

So you see, fat in your diet is not the cause of excess fat in your body any more than protein is. We must come right back to your consumption of glue-foods, the man-made carbohydrates, as the specific and exact cause of your excess fat.

Other functions of fat in your body

Besides providing a source of energy, fat performs a variety of other functions in your body. Here are some of the main reasons you need a certain amount of body fat:

Fat provides the right shape in the right places. Although you've probably never given much thought to fat and its relationship to appearance and beauty, fat is important to round out the body and give it extra padding in the right places.

A woman would not be beautiful without some fat: she'd be nothing but skin and bones; she'd have no sexy curves to cuddle. The ideal female figure has the proper distribution of just the right amount of fat.

Fat promotes normal growth. A pronounced deficiency of fat in the diet will bring about symptoms of malnutrition and starvation. People whose diets do not include enough fat are often undersized and greatly undernourished.

Fat keeps your skin clear, soft, and supple. If your skin had no fat cells in it, it would be dry and brittle, scaly and hard. Fat makes your skin soft, smooth, and supple. It gives you a clear complexion and helps provide good skin tone.

Contrary to what many people think, fat in the diet is not responsible for pimples, acne, or a bad complexion. Man-made carbohydrates, the glue-foods, are wholly responsible. The absence of natural fat in the diet actually compounds the problem.

Fat influences the rate at which your bones calcify. Calcium is one of the major minerals needed by your body. Unless you have enough calcium in your diet, your bones will not harden properly, and broken bones will not be repaired as they should be. Without the proper amount of fat in your diet, calcium cannot be absorbed and utilized by your body. As a result, calcification of your bone structure would be greatly impaired.

Without fat in your diet, you'd have a vitamin deficiency. Certain vitamins — A, D, and E — are fat-soluble. Unless there is fat in your diet, these vitamins cannot enter your body from your digestive tract. Even if you took vitamin supplements of A, D, and E, you'd still need fat in your diet before they could be absorbed from your digestive system. Fat is the vehicle these vitamins must use to get into your bloodstream and lymphatic vessels and on to the various parts of the body where they are needed.

The right kind of fat helps control your weight. I know it's hard to believe right now, but you need to eat the right kind of fat to get slim. I'll discuss this point in greater detail in Chapter 3.

Eliminating fat from your diet will lead to illness

The most striking example of this is shown in the case of a young Harvard anthropology professor, Viljalmur Stefansson, who spent an Arctic winter with the Eskimos, eating only their food.

The Eskimos lived entirely on a diet of fish washed down with oily water in which chunks of the fish had been briefly stewed. Stefansson's stomach rebelled at such primitive food.

He tried to improve it by broiling the fish, but when he did, he became weak and dizzy and suffered all the signs and symptoms of malnutrition and starvation. He realized that on this highly restricted diet his body had to have not only the protein in the fish, but also the fat and other nutrient materials that were leaked out into the water when the fish was stewed.

He finally did adjust psychologically to this diet, for it was either that or starve to death. During this winter with the Eskimos he had no man-made carbohydrates whatever. Yet at the end of that time he felt fine and was in excellent health.

Some time after this experience, Stefansson and a Dr. Anderson were sent to the Arctic by the American Museum of Natural History for a year of research. They were fitted out with every necessity including a full supply of "civilized foods," primarily the man-made carbohydrates. But they decided to live exactly as the natives of the Canadian Arctic did. This meant they had to exist on a hunter's diet – the fish they could catch, the game they could kill, the water they could find. They lived on a primitive diet of protein and fat just as man had lived before he learned to plant and harvest crops.

They found that when fat became scarce – as it did one time when they could not get seal oil and they ate only lean caribou meat without any additional fat – they became sick. They grew weak, dizzy, had headaches, and suffered all the signs and symptoms of malnutrition and starvation. But just as soon as oil was restored to their diet, they recovered.

Here are the results of some other diet experiments

Later, Stefansson took part in a diet experiment of New York City's Bellevue Hospital. The research team was headed by Dr. Eugene F. DuBois, at the time medical director of the Russell Sage Foundation. He later became chief physician at New York Hospital and Professor of Physiology at Cornell University's Medical College.

Again, Stefansson found that he got along well on a diet of meat and fat. He suffered only when fat was eliminated from his diet just as before. But the absence of man-made carbohydrates had only good effects.

At the end of this experiment, the research team reported that Stefansson had reduced to his best normal weight. He showed no deficiency symptoms. There was no loss of energy. In fact, he had much more energy than he had on a "normal" diet. He was in excellent health.

Dr. Blake F. Donaldson also conducted a famous experiment with obese patients in the New York hospital. He selected only specific people who'd never been able to reduce successfully before on low-calorie diets. He took the excess fat off these patients with a diet that was high in protein and fat, but had no man-made carbohydrates whatever.

The E. I. DuPont company headquarters in Wilmington, Delaware, ran a similar experiment on a group of its more corpulent executives who had been unable to reduce on low-calorie diets. Under the direction of Dr. Albert W. Pennington and Dr. George H. Gehrmann, director of DuPont's medical division, these individuals were given all the protein and fat they wanted, but they were allowed no man-made carbohydrates at all.

The results were excellent. Fat loss varied from person to person. So did the time each one required to reach his goal. However, when the group average was figured out, each dieter had lost 22 pounds in just slightly more than three months.

We can now draw several major conclusions from these various examples and experiments:

1. Man-made carbohydrates can be eliminated from your diet and you'll suffer no ill-effects whatever.
2. Proteins cannot be eliminated from your diet if you are to remain in good health.
3. If you eliminate fat from your diet, you will probably become ill.
4. Fat in your diet does not necessarily contribute to increased fat in your body.
5. When man-made carbohydrates are missing from your diet, your body uses fat for energy instead.
6. *Man-made carbohydrates cause your excess fat. Proteins and fats do not.*

Natural carbohydrates are non-glue-foods

Although all glue-foods are carbohydrates, not all carbohydrates are glue-foods. Natural carbohydrates are non-glue-foods. The two main sources of natural carbohydrates are fruits and vegetables.

Natural carbohydrates such as fresh fruits and vegetables do not cause excess fat, either. First of all, fruits and vegetables are not all sugar and starch as are the man-made carbohydrates. Fruits and vegetables have necessary cellulose and fiber. Secondly, natural carbohydrates are absorbed more slowly. There is no sudden upsurge of blood sugar from them as there is from the man-made carbohydrates — the glue-foods. So there is no need for your body to convert these natural sources of sugar and starch into permanent body fat for storage. Since they are digested more slowly, your body can use them the way they were meant to be used: to meet its current energy requirements.

Not only that, fresh fruits and vegetables are valuable to you for still another reason: they contain many of the natural vitamins and minerals your body needs to stay in good health.

You cannot overeat non-glue-foods

One of the first things my patients discover on my diet is that they have no desire to overeat the non-glue-foods as they did the glue-foods. You'll find the same thing happens to you, too.

"Before I went on your non-glue-food diet, I was always eating," Neal told me. "I just never could seem to get enough. I always had a bloated, full, and stuffed feeling, yet I still wanted more to eat.

"On your non-glue-food diet, Doc, I find I eat a lot less than I used to. I mean, the foods on your diet seem to be so satisfying and filling, I don't have that constant desire to eat that I used to have. I think your non-glue-food diet is really great."

You see, your body has a built-in *appestat* that keeps you from overeating non-glue-foods. If you look over the list of proteins — eggs, cheese, fish, seafood, meat, poultry — you'll see that you can eat only so much of them before your body simply refuses to accept any more. Your built-in body appestat knows when you've had enough and it lets you know that in no uncertain terms.

The same thing can be said for fat foods. You will most definitely know when you eat too many fatty foods, for you'll become slightly nauseated and feel sick to your stomach. Again, your built-in appestat lets you know when enough is enough.

Your appestat also works to help control your intake of fresh fruits and vegetables. Your body will tolerate just so many apples or oranges or grapefruit at any one time before it rebels. Then you become so full of them, you cannot possibly eat any more. The same is true of fresh vegetables: corn; peas; beans; Brussels sprouts; cabbage; asparagus; and others.

How our appestats react to glue-foods

However, our appestats do not seem to work to help us control our intake of man-made carbohydrates — the glue-foods. Why not? Probably because it has not developed fast enough in its ability to handle our *civilized glue-foods*. It is capable of handling a primitive diet, but it is not yet prepared to take on our modern man-made carbohydrates.

In prehistoric times, people lived primarily on a diet of meat — much as the Eskimos still do — and that's what our bodies were built to handle. For millions of years the human body had to deal with only small amounts of carbohydrates, and these were primarily the unrefined natural carbohydrates of fresh fruits and fresh vegetables.

When man learned to till the soil, he shifted slowly from a hunter's diet to a primitive farmer's diet, and the amount of carbohydrates he ate increased, but they were still largely unrefined. It's only since the beginning of this century that man-made carbohydrates have increased so rapidly in quantity and availability.

So the body appestat that was originally designed to metabolize proteins, fats, and the natural carbohydrates of fresh fruits and fresh vegetables has finally broken down in those of us who are fat from our overconsumption of cake and cookies, candy and ice cream — the glue-foods.

In all my years of practice and treating people with weight problems, *I have never met a person who became fat from overeating any of the non-glue-foods* — the proteins, fats, or natural carbohydrates. The fat person always gets fat because he overeats the man-made carbohydrates — the glue-foods.

Lorene's experience

"The moment I stopped eating glue-foods, I started losing weight," Lorene told me. "And the loss was really dramatic. I never in all my life thought a person could lose so much weight so fast and still feel good.

"I've lost more than 50 pounds in six months on your non-glue-food diet, Doctor, and I feel absolutely marvelous. There's just no way to compare how I feel now with the way I felt before. Now I'm alive; I'm a thousand percent better!"

11 reasons why the non-glue-food diet will work for you

In conclusion, then, here are 11 reasons why my

non-glue-food diet will work for you to help you get rid of your excess fat quickly, safely, easily, and permanently.

1. The non-glue-food diet eliminates the cause of your excess fat. Other diets do not.
2. When you get rid of the cause of your excess fat, your weight loss will be permanent.
3. On the non-glue-food diet you lose your excess fat — not your vital muscle tissue.
4. On the non-glue-food diet you avoid only the glue-foods that make you fat.
5. When you don't eat glue-foods, hunger stays away longer.
6. You don't have to starve yourself; you're never hungry.
7. Generally speaking, you can eat all the meat, poultry, fish and seafood, dairy products, fresh fruits and fresh vegetables you want.
8. You can still satisfy your sweet tooth.
9. You don't have to use willpower on this diet.
10. You'll not become exhausted, worn out, fatigued, irritable and nervous, or lose all your energy on the non-glue-food diet. In fact, you'll find you have much more energy.
11. You can maintain this diet indefinitely without any danger whatever to your health. To tell the truth, as you lose your excess fat, you'll gain back your good health.

I've given you this background of glue-foods and non-glue-foods and how your body uses them so you'll not start on my non-glue-food diet without knowing what you're doing or why you're doing it.

I want you to know how the non-glue-food diet works, why it works, and how it'll help get rid of your excess fat.

3. How to use the non-glue-food diet to lose all your excess fat no matter how much you weigh now

This chapter is broken down into two major sections for your convenience. Section I is primarily for people who have 20 pounds or less of excess fat to lose. Section II is for those who have more than 20 pounds to lose.

However, even if you have more than 20 pounds of excess fat to get rid of, you should still read Section I before going on to Section II, for all the information it contains will apply to you except for the rule that tells you to eat all the fresh fruits and vegetables you want.

If you have 20 pounds or less of excess fat to get rid of, the non-glue-food diet you'll find in Section I is just right for you. It will let you lose from two to three pounds each week. In just ten weeks — perhaps even less — you can lose all your excess fat so you will be down to your ideal weight painlessly, easily, and without any extra effort whatever.

Not everyone has 40 or more pounds to lose. Some of my patients have only 20 or less pounds to get rid of. But the loss of 20 pounds on the non-glue-food diet is just as important to them as it is to the person who's excessively overweight.

For example, as Nancy told me, "I feel better than I have for ten years, Doctor. I've been on and off various diets for years, but your non-glue-food diet is the only one that's ever been able to take my excess weight off and keep it off."

Nancy was 20 pounds overweight when she came to see me. She got rid of every bit of her excess fat in just six weeks. If you're quite a bit overweight, 20 pounds might not seem like much to you, but to a smaller person, that's a lot of extra fat to be carrying around. If you don't think so, next time you're in the grocery store, pick up a 20 pound sack of potatoes and hold it in your arms for five minutes or carry it around the store by one hand while you're shopping. You'll soon see what I mean.

Now if you do have more than 20 pounds of excess fat to lose — or if you have less to get rid of, but you happen to be in a big hurry for some especially good reason — then you should follow the extra rules that are given to you in Section II. By using this slightly stricter version of the non-glue-food diet, you'll be able to lose from four to five pounds each week. Naturally, the more pounds you have to lose, the longer it will take, but you can still get down to your ideal weight easily, painlessly, and without any extra effort at all. Look at Max, for example.

How Max and Thelma reached their goals

Max and Thelma, a husband and wife who were both patients of mine, decided to go on my non-glue-food diet together. Thelma was 19 pounds overweight; Max was carrying around 38 pounds of excess fat. Both got down to their ideal weight, but not in the same length of time.

Thelma used the non-glue-food diet in Section I and was down to her best weight in seven weeks. Max used the diet in

Section II, Part 1, and reached his ideal weight in 11 weeks.

"I thought it would take me twice as long as Thelma to get rid of my excess weight because I was twice as fat," Max told me. "But it didn't. It only took four more weeks because of the different diet version you recommended for me."

You see, it doesn't really matter how much you weigh. You can still get rid of all your excess fat, for there's a diet version in this chapter that's just right for you.

The author's experience losing weight

For instance, I myself had 45 pounds of excess fat to get rid of. I lost 12 pounds of it in the first month by using the diet directions in Section I. Then my fat loss slowed down and I knew I had to do something else.

As you will recall, I experimented on myself first with this non-glue-food diet. Through this experimentation, I came up with the additional information that's given in Section II of this chapter, for people who have more than 20 pounds of excess fat to lose. I used the diet in Part 1 of Section II to get rid of the rest of my excess fat − 33 more pounds − and by the end of that first year, I was down to 147 from 192. I've stayed between 147 and 152 ever since without any trouble whatever simply by following the easy instructions in the last chapter, which tells how to maintain your ideal weight after you've once reached it.

"One of the wonderful things about the non-glue-food diet is that it's so easy to maintain your ideal weight after you've reached it," Harriet told me. "I've never had any desire to go back to eating glue-foods again. I've found that the non-glue-food diet is always sufficient to keep me feeling comfortable and satisfied. I'm never going to be fat again, Doctor, thanks to you."

If I can do it and my fat patients can do it without any trouble, then you can do it, too. I have never seen a single patient of mine fail to lose all his excess fat just as long as he thoroughly and conscientiously followed the non-glue-food diet's few simple and easy rules.

The non-glue-food diet is neither
a crash diet nor a starvation diet

You didn't put on your excess weight overnight, so don't try to take it off overnight. The non-glue-food diet will not do that for you, nor should you expect it to.

The non-glue-food diet is not a crash diet or starvation diet. That kind of diet is always associated with Melba toast and black coffee for breakfast, and as far as I'm concerned, that's a miserable way to start a day. I'm sure you feel the same way, too.

On the non-glue-food diet you will not lose all your excess fat in one week, either, but you will get rid of it steadily, gradually, and surely. My non-glue-food diet will help you lose all your excess fat safely, naturally, and permanently without any of the dangers or risks you run on a crash diet or a starvation diet.

How to let your body set its own rate of loss

Whatever rate of fat loss your body assumes on the non-glue-food diet is the proper rate for you. If it takes a little longer than you think it should, don't become discouraged. Americans are the most impatient people in the world. Once they make up their minds to do something, they always want it done yesterday, if not sooner. Just be patient; I know you'll be successful.

I have found, however, that on the non-glue-food diet, patients of mine with 20 pounds or less of excess fat to get rid of will lose an average of two to three pounds each week. Those with more than 20 pounds of excess fat will lose an average of four or five pounds each week by using a slightly different version of my original non-glue-food diet.

When you've lost all your excess fat, you will stop losing weight. Your body will regulate itself. It will stabilize at the proper level. You cannot starve yourself on the non-glue-food diet, for on it you will lose only your excess fat, not your vital muscle tissue.

Of course, you won't lose all the fat tissue in your body. You shouldn't. You'll get rid of only the excess. A certain amount of fat (eleven percent of your body's ideal weight) is necessary for good health.

Benefits you'll gain

When you reach your ideal weight, you'll have more energy, more vitality, more pep and go-power. You'll be able to enjoy the benefits of being slim, trim, and in tip-top shape. Your complexion will be clear; your hair will shine. You'll be free from aches and pains. You'll be regular without laxatives; you'll even sleep better. And no matter how old you are, your sex life will definitely improve. You see, fat cells in your body have no sensory nerve endings. In fact, too much fat, no matter where it is, can interfere with your sense of touch. Excess fat on your abdomen, legs, thighs, and breasts blocks off much of the sensual satisfaction of sexual intercourse. The multitudinous fat cells physically get in the way of the sensitive tactile nerve endings that give you sexual pleasure, enjoyment, and satisfaction.

SECTION I: How to Lose Two or Three Pounds Each Week

Section I applies to you if you have *20 pounds or less* of excess fat to lose. However, even if you do have more than 20 pounds to get rid of, you should still read this section, for you can use all the information it contains except the rule that states that you can eat all the fresh fruits and vegetables you want. Not only that, when you do get down to less than 20 pounds of excess fat, you can switch over to this section from Section II, and use it to finish up.

Here, then, is the first easy rule for you to follow:

Eliminate all the glue-foods from your diet

To refresh your memory, let me remind you that a glue-food is any man-made carbohydrate food that contains sugar, flour, or starch that has been added, increased, or changed in any way during the manufacturing process. Glue-foods will include — but are not necessarily limited to —

1. Sugar, flour, or starch as individual items;
2. Soft drinks, candy, ice cream;
3. All cereals and cereal products, including rice;
4. Cake, cupcakes, cookies, pie, puddings;
5. All desserts made with sugar, flour, or cornstarch;
6. All canned or stewed fruit cooked with sugar or syrup;
7. All fruit frozen in sugar, for example, strawberries;
8. Canned or frozen vegetables that have been creamed, for instance, creamed corn or creamed peas;
9. All potatoes (white, sweet, and yams), potato chips, or other potato products;
10. All pasta, for example, spaghetti, macaroni, noodles;
11. All soups except bouillon;
12. All dried fruits such as dates, figs, raisins, prunes;
13. Bakery products or homemade baked goods such as bread, biscuits, crackers, rolls, doughnuts, and other pastries;
14. Pancakes, waffles, and french toast;
15. All beer, ale, and sweet wines;
16. Miscellaneous items such as chewing gum, honey, jam, jelly, pickle relishes, sweet pickles, syrup, and yogurt with fruit;
17. Any food I've not specifically mentioned here that has sugar, flour, or starch added, increased, or changed in any way during the manufacturing process.

Now I've tried to close all the loopholes by adding number 17 to this list of specific glue-foods to avoid. But I'm sure there must still be a variety of glue-foods I don't even know about. After all, I'm from the Midwest, and I'm not completely familiar with the more sophisticated food tastes of people in large metropolitan centers. So if you do happen to know of some other glue-food containing sugar, flour, or starch, and I've not included it here, please add it to this list of specific glue-foods to avoid.

If you don't do that, you'll not be cheating me. You'll be cheating no one but yourself. But I also know this: if you don't lose your excess fat as fast as you think you should, you'll not blame yourself at all; you'll blame me. So please don't cheat. Again I say, I have never seen a person fail to lose all his excess fat as long as he thoroughly and conscientiously follows my non-glue-food diet.

Once in a while I will treat a patient who doesn't lose as much weight as he should. If at the end of a couple of weeks there's been no change, I sit down with him to discuss his problem again. Close questioning usually reveals that he has not been following my non-glue-food diet properly.

At that point I tell him he must make a decision. If he really wants to reduce, lose weight, and regain his health — wonderful. I want to help him. But if he's not serious about wanting to reduce, I no longer want him as a patient. So many other people want to be helped that I cannot waste my time on someone who isn't serious about losing weight.

If you think you might have a hard time remembering the specific foods on this list, I can simplify it even further for you. All you need do is remember this one major rule: *eat nothing that has been canned, dried, packaged, or precooked.*

Such a rule would limit you to fresh meat, fresh fruit, and fresh vegetables. You couldn't go wrong following this rule, for then you couldn't possibly eat any foods that contain man-made carbohydrates in the form of sugar, flour, or starch.

Eat all the protein foods you want

If you will remember what you learned about proteins in the last chapter, you'll know that they are never used as a source of energy except in an emergency, such as starvation. This, by the way, is one of the very real dangers of a low-calorie crash diet. Your body protein is used for immediate energy requirements and you end up losing vital muscle tissue instead of excess body fat.

"I always worried about going on a diet because I was afraid I'd end up with loose flabby skin on my arms and legs and under my chin," Opal said to me. "But that didn't happen on your non-glue-food diet, Doctor. I lost 68 pounds and maybe I ought to be flabby, but I'm not. My skin isn't loose and my arms and legs still feel firm and well packed, but now they're packed with healthy lean meat, not with fat."

Remember that protein is used to build muscle tissue, blood, and bone. That's why the non-glue-food diet is so successful in getting rid of fat without causing you to lose your vital muscle tissue. Plenty of protein prevents flabbiness and loose skin and helps build new lean meat to replace your lost fat tissue.

Any diet that eliminates or reduces your protein intake to help you get rid of your excess fat is a false and dangerous fad diet. You must have protein to repair and replace your vital muscle tissue, blood, and bone. Protein in your diet is absolutely necessary for good health.

Excellent sources of animal protein are eggs, cheese, fish, seafood, meats such as beef, lamb, ham, pork, and poultry of all kinds. Processed meats such as sausage, pepperoni, salami, weiners, and cold cuts (except cold sliced ham) should not be eaten. Although they do contain protein, they also contain such fillers as sugar, starch, flour, meal, and so on. Just read the label and you'll see what I mean.

Proteins are never converted into permanent body fat

You can eat all the protein foods you want without any fear of building up your excess body fat. If you don't believe that, try overeating them some time. You can't do it. Your body appestat won't allow you to overeat the non-glue-foods such as meat, eggs, cheese, fish, and seafood. You'll get sick at your stomach and have to give up long before you could eat enough of them to get fat.

In fact, if you will just avoid the glue-foods, you'll lose almost all of your excess fat, and it won't matter one bit how much protein food you eat.

Eat all the fresh, frozen, or canned fruits and vegetables you want

Now if you have more than 20 pounds of excess fat to get rid of, this is the one rule in this section that will not apply to you. Unfortunately, you cannot eat all the fresh, frozen, or canned fruits and vegetables you want. You'll have to turn to Section II to find out which ones you'll be allowed to eat.

However, even so, don't stop reading this rule just yet. When you do get down to less than 20 pounds of excess fat, you can switch over to this rule from Section II and use it to finish up.

Generally speaking, if you have 20 pounds or less of excess fat to lose, you can eat all the fresh, frozen, or canned fruits and vegetables that you want to eat. Of course, canned goods that have sugar, flour, or starch added, increased, or changed during the manufacturing process are not allowed as you already know. These are the glue-foods that you must avoid.

Fruits

For instance, fruit canned or stewed in sugar or syrup has become a man-made carbohydrate. So have strawberries, blueberries, or any other fruit that has been frozen in sugar.

While we're discussing fruit, let's take a look at fruit juices. You may drink any fruit juice you want: orange juice, grape juice, grapefruit juice, apple juice, just as long as no sugar has been added for sweetening.

For instance, I prefer unsweetened grapefruit juice since it has much less natural carbohydrate than orange, grape, or apple juice. If unsweetened grapefruit juice is a little more than you can take, especially at the beginning, you can always use some saccharin or artificial sugar to sweeten it up.

Although tomato juice is considered a vegetable juice, I'll

mention it here, for it is a good breakfast juice. It is lower in natural carbohydrate than any fruit juice, and it is also extremely high in its vitamin C content.

Some of my patients never cared for fruit before they went on my non-glue-food diet. The elimination of sweet and fattening glue-foods has given them a desire to eat wholesome fresh fruit they never had before.

"I'll reach for an apple or an orange every time now instead of doughnuts or cookies or cake," says Pamela. "And why shouldn't I? Since I've been doing that on your non-glue-food diet, Doctor, I've lost 23 pounds. I don't want it back!"

Vegetables

Now then, vegetables. Creamed peas, creamed corn, or any other creamed vegetables, whether canned or frozen, move from the permitted list to the glue-food category, because of the thickening. Just read the label on the box or the can. You'll know for yourself if it's a glue-food or not.

Exceptions

There is one other big exception to this general rule that you can eat all the fruits and vegetables that you want. Although I've already included it on the list of glue-foods to avoid, you really ought to know why it's there.

First of all, let me say that no matter what good, sound rules are laid down in accordance with definite scientific principles, there will always be a few exceptions that refuse to fall into line and fit the pattern. And that is true here, too.

That one exception to the general rule here is that you should not eat any white potatoes, sweet potatoes, or yams. In fact, *you should not eat potatoes or potato products of any kind,* and that includes potato chips, too.

Other than that one major exception, you can eat all the other vegetables you want to unless they've been turned into glue-foods by sugar, flour, or starch, as I mentioned a little while ago.

I have patients tell me they never learned to really appreciate fresh green vegetables until they went on my non-glue-food diet. Glue-foods had deadened their tastebuds for the nourishing and healthful non-glue-foods.

"I used to be nothing but a 'meat, bread, and potatoes' eater," Paul told me. "I never cared for asparagus or broccoli, cauliflower or cabbage, anything like that. After a few months on your diet, Doc, I find I'm extremely well satisfied with them. Besides, losing 43 pounds is a tremendous incentive to learn to like fresh green vegetables."

Why are potatoes a glue-food?

Potatoes are an exceptionally rich source of natural carbohydrate, much richer than leafy green vegetables in starch, for example. However, that's not the main reason they're excluded from the list of vegetables you can eat. The main reason you should not eat potatoes is that the average person always eats such large helpings of them.

When you eat large helpings of potatoes, you push them right into the glue-food category. An excessive amount of potatoes will react in your body exactly as a man-made carbohydrate does.

Remember that when you eat more glue-foods than your body needs for *immediate energy,* your blood sugar goes above its normal limits. That excess sugar in your blood must always be converted into permanent fat at once or be spilled over into the urine. *That's what happens when you eat too many potatoes at one time.*

All types of potato servings put on weight

Most restaurants or sandwich shops today offer French fried potatoes with your hamburger. And naturally, you order French fries with your hamburger sandwich, don't you? I can't imagine you ordering a hamburger with asparagus or cabbage or green beans.

Some eating places offer you fish and *chips,* the English version of french fries. And when you go out for a steak dinner, don't you usually get a great big baked potato to go along with it? You do if you eat at the Bonanza Sirloin Pit or the Ponderosa or the Ranchhouse or whatever the name of your favorite steak place is.

All these steak houses push their baked potatoes just as the hamburger places push French fries. In fact, just the other day I picked up a magazine and I saw that one steak-house chain has gone so far as to advertise their baked potato as if it were their main dish. Their ad said in effect, "You can order our delicious baked potato for only $1.79 or so, and get a Western Cut Steak, a tossed salad, and a hot buttered roll to go with it."

In a Midwest restaurant, a hot roast beef or pork sandwich loaded down with lots of mashed potatoes and gravy over two thick slices of bread is still a favorite with many an Iowa or Missouri farmer when he eats in town.

There's more profit in potatoes than in anything else in a restaurant. They're used as a filler. My father-in-law ran an extremely successful cafe for more than 25 years and he often told me he'd never have made it had it not been for the profit in potatoes.

And at home the average family also uses potatoes as a filler just as they do bread. Meat, bread, and potatoes form the *basic three foods* for the average family's meal with most of the emphasis on potatoes and bread. In extremely poor families beans take the place of meat.

I was born and raised on an Iowa farm and we had potatoes with every meal including breakfast. In fact, a real farm breakfast without potatoes is almost unheard of where I come from.

Potatoes are to an American what rice is to the Oriental. If bread is the poor man's protein, the potato is the poor man's vegetable, for it is the cheapest one there is.

So that's why potatoes are placed in the glue-food category. We simply eat too many of them too often and as a result, they act just like a man-made carbohydrate in our bodies.

"I never miss potatoes at all," Dick said to me. "That's hard to believe for I used to eat them with every meal: hash browns for breakfast; french fries or mashed potatoes for lunch; baked potatoes for supper. Doc, I ate potatoes all day long.

"I don't know how much of my excess 53 pounds was due to eating too many potatoes, and I don't really care. All that really matters is that I'm down to my ideal weight now on your non-glue-food diet and I'm going to stay there, so no more potatoes for me!"

Once you stop eating potatoes, it won't be long before you won't miss them either. So much of what we do in life is habit and it's just as easy to form the habit of not eating potatoes as it is to form the habit of eating them. Besides, the benefits of not eating them are too good to pass up.

For even faster weight loss results, use the "three-to-one" rule

"Doc, is there any way I can speed up my loss of excess fat without cutting down on the total amount of fruit or vegetables I'm eating now?" one of my fat patients asked.

"There sure is, Henry," I said. "You can use the *Three-to-One Rule*. It will help you get rid of your excess fat even faster than you're losing it now."

If you'd like to speed up your fat loss, too, just as Henry did, but without cutting down on the total amount of food you're eating right now, or without resorting to the stricter version of the non-glue-food diet you'll find in the next section, then the Three-to-One Rule is just the thing for you.

You see, leafy vegetables such as lettuce, broccoli, asparagus, Brussels sprouts, cabbage, and so on have much more cellulose and fiber than do peas, navy beans, kidney and pinto beans, blackeyed peas, and corn. Therefore, they have far less natural carbohydrate, too.

Although the natural carboyhdrates in fresh fruits and vegetables do not normally contribute to excess fat, remember that your carbohydrate metabolism is not normal. It is abnormal; that's why you're fat. Anything you can do, then, to keep from triggering your pancreas to produce insulin and turn carbohydrate in your blood stream into permanent body fat is to your advantage. That's why it's important at this stage in your diet to do all you can to keep even the natural carbohydrates at a low level in your blood stream.

So it stands to reason that if you eat more of the leafy vegetables than you do of the seed or kernel type to keep your natural carbohydrate intake low, you'll lose your excess fat even faster.

What the three-to-one rule does for you

To make sure you do this, simply use the three-to-one rule this way. Eat three times as much of the leafy vegetables as you do of the seed or kernel type. For example, if you have corn and broccoli for dinner, you should eat three bites of broccoli to every one bite of corn. That's all there is to it, but it's an extremely effective way to speed up your loss of excess fat.

The Three-to-One Rule will keep you from eating an excessive amount of the high carbohydrate vegetables like corn, peas, blackeyed peas, all kinds of beans such as navy, lima, pinto, and kidney.

By eating more of the leafy vegetables, you'll take in a smaller amount of natural carbohydrates. At the same time, you'll feel physically full for you'll be filling your digestive tract with more cellulose and fiber.

"The Three-to-One Rule is one of the best methods I've found to keep from eating too many high carbohydrate vegetables," Keith told me. "You know after I lost my first 18 pounds, I seemed to stagnate for a while. Then you told me about the Three-to-One Rule and I was able to easily drop another 12 pounds in just a few weeks. It's really worthwhile, Doc."

Drink all you want of these beverages

I've already discussed the fruit juices you are allowed to have. In addition to them, you may drink all you want of water, mineral water, club soda, sugar-free diet soda or cola, beef or chicken broth or bouillon and tea.

Ketones require water

One point that is well worth mentioning here is that when you burn up your body's excess fat, you'll be excreting ketone bodies — a waste product of fat metabolism — in your urine.

These ketone bodies are actually fatty acids and can cause your urine to sting and burn slightly. This is absolutely nothing to be concerned about. If you can drink from six to eight glasses of water daily, you will dilute these ketone bodies and they'll be less irritating to the mucous membranes of your urinary tract.

If you cannot drink that many glasses of water in a day, don't worry about it. Drink as much as your thirst requires. Don't restrict your fluid intake, but don't force it either.

Avoid or limit these beverages

You should avoid, as I've already mentioned on the glue-food list, soft drinks that contain sugar, beer, ale, and sweet wines.

Coffee should be limited to no more than six cups a day and I would prefer that you drink far less than that for several reasons.

First of all, coffee does contain some carbohydrate. Second, the caffein in coffee is a stimulant and it tends to make you jumpy and nervous. This is not good, especially when you're going all out to get rid of your excess fat.

I used to drink a great deal of coffee all day long. Now I limit myself to one cup each morning with my breakfast. I recommend strongly that you do the same.

I feel, although I cannot prove it scientifically, that more coffee than that irritates my stomach, upsets my digestion, and tends to give me a slight diarrhea. At any rate, now that I limit my coffee to no more than one cup a day at breakfast time, I no longer have those symptoms of digestive distress.

Milk is a wonderful all-around food. It contains protein, fat, and natural carbohydrate. Unfortunately, it has too much carbohydrate for your pancreas to handle right now. So until you're down to your ideal weight, or close to it, it would be best for you not to drink any milk at all.

Dressings and garnishes you can use freely

Of course, you'll have to avoid any salad dressings that contain sugar. However, you don't have to eat your salads raw without any dressing at all as so many diets demand that you do.

You can use oil and vinegar, Roquefort and Caesar dressings. You can also add crumbled bacon bits, anchovies, fried pork rinds, grated cheese, chopped hard-boiled eggs, mushrooms, and sour cream.

Onions, peppers, olives, and sour or dill pickles can also be added to make your salads more zestful and appetizing.

You can use these condiments for seasoning

You can use salt, pepper, prepared or dry mustard, horseradish, vinegar, vanilla and other extracts, artificial sweeteners, and any dry herb or spice that contains no sugar.

Most steak sauces and catsup contain sugar and should not be used until you're down to your ideal weight. For years I ate my steaks without catsup or steak sauce for I preferred to taste only the meat. I didn't want the good meat flavor spoiled with sauce. Then I went on my diet and for the first time, I wanted steak sauce and catsup just because I couldn't have any. But that's human nature for you.

If you've been covering your steaks with catsup and steak sauce, eat them without any seasoning other than salt and pepper and I know you'll soon discover you've been disguising the good natural beef taste with a lot of man-made junk. Before long I know you'll prefer your meat without any sauce whatever.

How to establish a sensible eating pattern as soon as possible

Most of us work better and feel better when our lives follow a definite fixed plan and pattern. This is also true of our eating habits as well. Try to regulate your meals so that you eat at approximately the same time every day. A fixed pattern of meals and a regular schedule — whether you eat three, six, or whatever — will help your body chemistry adjust more quickly to your new diet.

Even your own internal body chemistry gets into certain fixed habits. It learns to expect food at definite times and intervals. If you skip a meal or eat late, you'll upset your own internal normal body cycles.

So many fat people have the bad habit of skipping breakfast and eating a light lunch, thinking and hoping they'll lose some weight. Then they load themselves down with a heavy supper meal because they are ravenously hungry from going too long without food. But by then the day's energy requirements are nearly over so almost everything they eat at supper time turns to excess body fat.

You'd be far better off to eat a bigger breakfast of high protein foods to give you lasting energy for the morning — a bigger lunch, again of high protein foods, so you'll have plenty of energy for the afternoon — and a light supper when you're through for the day.

Meal frequency

I always insist that my fat patients eat at least three balanced meals a day. *I would prefer that they use six smaller meals to consume the amount of food they would normally eat in those three meals.* However, I realize that this could be extremely inconvenient and impractical — perhaps even impossible for some — especially when the person is eating his meals with other members of the family, so I don't insist on this. However, if you could eat the same amount of food in six smaller meals that you would normally eat in three larger meals, *you will lose your excess fat even faster.*

Why is that? Well, we're right back to the principle of eating only the amount of food you actually need for immediate energy. Remember the excess carbohydrate that is not needed for immediate energy will always be turned into permanent body fat.

I have found that those of my patients who are able to eat six smaller meals a day lose their excess fat even faster than those who eat the same amount in three meals a day. They also seem to be more satisfied on six smaller meals a day than on three larger ones. Comparisons are difficult, of course, for no two bodies are exactly alike and no two people eat exactly the same food.

But just for example, Harrison L., an insurance executive told me, "Glue-foods and big meals must have been the cause of my middle-age paunch. Now after eight weeks on your non-glue-food diet eating six smaller meals a day, it's all gone."

Eat whenever you're hungry

Although I do want you to establish a definite and fixed eating pattern as soon as you can, you should never go hungry just because it's not yet time for you to eat. Your stomach is a far better timepiece to gauge your hunger by than any clock will ever be.

So, if you are hungry, eat. Never allow yourself to become overly hungry. Don't skip a meal. If you eat between meals though, eat some high protein foods such as cheese, meat, or seafood. Or eat some fresh fruit instead of glue-foods like doughnuts, pie, cake, or ice cream. And don't eat until you're stuffed. *Eat just enough to take the edge off your hunger.*

"On your non-glue-food diet, I eat more often, but I don't stuff myself any more," Roberta told me. "I've learned to eat just enough to satisfy my hunger without feeling overly full. I've lost 34 pounds that way, and do I feel better!"

Don't eat when you're not hungry

Although you should always eat when you're hungry, you should never eat when you're not hungry just from force of habit, the lack of something to do, or to be sociable.

The most fattening food of the day is the glue-food you eat after supper while you're watching TV. And the thing is, you're probably not even hungry, for none of that food is needed for immediate energy. How could it be needed for energy when you're not doing anything to burn the food?

Most of what you eat after the last meal of the day is eaten purely out of habit, to satisfy your sweet tooth, or the need for something to do. If you do eat in the evening, never eat a glue-food. You'll undo everything you've accomplished during the day.

If you must eat after supper, then, reach for a high protein food such as a piece of cheese or meat. *If you're not hungry enough to eat one of those foods, then you're not really hungry.* You're just eating something from force of habit or lack of something to do, so you'd be better off to skip it entirely.

"My snacks during the day and in the evening while watching TV were always pie and ice cream, cake, cookies, and a coke," Cindy said. "And they weren't really snacks either. They were literally full-sized meals of glue-food.

"Now I eat some meat — fried chicken or roast beef or cold sliced ham — along with some deviled eggs and a big chunk of Cheddar cheese. I've found it takes far less of these non-glue-foods to satisfy me and I have a lot more zip and energy than I had before when I was munching away on glue-foods all the time."

Cindy still snacks a lot, as she says, but even so, she's taken off over 40 pounds while doing it. The thing is, you can't get fat on high protein non-glue-foods, no matter how hard you try.

How to satisfy your sweet tooth

The best way to really satisfy your sweet tooth is to eat fresh fruit. Fresh strawberries and raspberries are delicious for dessert. You can use milk or cream with artificial sweeteners instead of sugar.

Besides, it won't be long before you lose all your desire for hot fudge sundaes, pie or cake a la mode, and that sort of gooey glue-food. In fact, after you eat the natural fruits of the non-glue-food diet for only a short while, the taste of rich man-made carbohydrates will make you horribly sick at your stomach.

"I didn't think I'd ever lose my desire for sweet desserts," Fran said to me, "but I have. If you'd have told me 6 months ago, Doctor, that I'd pass up banana cream pie or a chocolate nut sundae for a piece of Cheddar cheese and some cold sliced ham or a can of tuna, I'd have said you were stark raving mad. But it's happened and I feel 30 pounds better than before I started on your non-glue-food diet. No one needs to feel sorry for me. I feel sorry for fat people who think they just have to eat those fattening glue-foods."

Actually, sweetness is all a matter of relativity. For instance, when I first started drinking unsweetened grapefruit juice, it tasted terribly sour to me. I used to sweeten it with saccharin. Today, unsweetened grapefruit juice actually tastes sweet to me for now I've become accustomed to it.

To speed up your fat loss, add polyunsaturated fats to your diet

It has been shown by scientifically controlled studies of obese patients that when *polyunsaturated fats* are added to their diets, the loss of permanent excess fat in the body through catabolism (breaking down) and oxidation (burning up) will be speeded up by 20 to 25 percent.

It is not completely known why polyunsaturated fats in the diet speed up the catabolism and oxidation of permanent excess fat in your body. Physiologists and biochemists do not yet understand all the intricate and detailed functions of the human body.

Somehow, polyunsaturated fats in the diet seem to act like kindling to start the fires burning in your body that consume your excess stored fat. However it works, it really does work.

I'm reminded of something here that Carl S. once told me about Alcoholics Anonymous. It seems to apply quite well, I think. "Most people coming to AA for the first time always want to know how Alcoholics Anonymous can keep them sober," Carl says. "They always want to know how the program works. I always tell them I don't know how it works for sure, but I do know this much: *It works fine.*"

The same thing holds true here. I can't tell you exactly how polyunsaturated fats in the diet help burn up the excess fat in your body. I can't tell you precisely how it works, but I can tell you this much for sure: *It works fine.*

Types of polyunsaturates

I always ask all my fat patients to add polyunsaturated fats such as safflower oil, corn oil, soybean oil, or olive oil — whatever strikes their own particular taste and fancy — to their noon and evening meals.

They usually use these oils in salads of fresh greens and on their leafy green vegetables. You can do the same. You can also increase your polyunsaturated fat intake by using margarine in place of butter and vegetable oils instead of lard and other animal fats in your cooking.

The key substance found in vegetable oil supplements is linoleic acid. The vegetable oils with the greatest quantity of linoleic acid are the most valuable in helping burn up the excess fat in your body and in keeping your blood cholesterol low as well. Safflower oil is the best of all such vegetable oils for it is 75 percent linoleic acid.

Why safflower oil is the best concentrated supplement

Besides using polyunsaturated fats in your cooking and on your salads and vegetables, you can also take safflower oil in a capsule form. No prescription is needed from your doctor to buy safflower oil capsules. You can find them at almost any good health food store.

They also contain Vitamin B_6, a potent factor in the catabolism and oxidation of your excess fat. Safflower oil capsules will help you rid your body of excess fat and keep your cholesterol level down at the same time.

I still take one 1150 milligram safflower oil capsule with each meal even though I'm no longer cursed with excess fat as I once was. However, I know from experience this safflower oil capsule will help keep any excess fat from forming in my body.

During the time I was taking off my 45 pounds of excess fat, I took up to 3 safflower oil capsules with each meal for a total of 9 each day.

Safflower oil capsules are also a source of energy

Safflower oil capsules furnish a slow burning, long lasting source of energy for you. They also play an important part in keeping your hunger pangs away, for they digest much more slowly than the man-made carbohydrates. Therefore, you're not perpetually hungry as you are when you eat glue-foods.

Since safflower oil capsules do furnish this steady flow of energy to your body, you'll be less likely to suffer an energy lag between meals. In fact, after you adjust to a diet rich in unsaturated fats instead of the glue-foods, you'll probably find that your need for *heavy* snacks between meals will either diminish or completely disappear.

I always recommend to all my fat patients that they take safflower oil capsules with each meal, too, for this concentrated source of polyunsaturated fat will help them speed up their loss of excess fat and give them extra energy at the same time.

I personally use the safflower oil capsules manufactured by the Radiance Products Company of Alhambra, California. If they are not available in your health food store, ask the proprietor to give you another good reliable brand. Just make sure you get the 1150 milligram size.

Safflower intake

You can start out by taking one capsule with each meal. If you seem to get abnormally hungry before you eat again, take two capsules with each meal. If you still think you get too hungry before you eat again or if your energy seems to sag, then take 3 capsules. There should be no reason to go any higher than 3 capsules per meal. That will give you a total of 9 each day and that should be enough.

Another good rule of thumb to follow in determining the number of safflower oil capsules to take with each meal is this: If you have 20 pounds or less of excess fat to lose, take 1 capsule with each meal. If you have between 20 and 40 pounds to get rid of, take 2 capsules with each meal. If you have more than 40 pounds of excess fat to lose, then you can take 3 capsules per meal.

Don't worry about taking in too much polyunsaturated fat in your diet. Your body will quickly let you know if that does happen. You'll simply become slightly nauseated. The worst that can happen to you is that you might get a rather loose bowel movement. If either of these do occur, don't get alarmed. Simply cut back one capsule at a time until you hit just the right number for you.

However, you should not go below one capsule with each main meal of the day until you're rid of all your excess fat. In fact, even after you're down to your ideal weight, you can keep taking one capsule with each meal. That's what I do just to keep the fat from forming again and to supply myself with a constant, steady, and reliable source of energy.

If at any time you know you're going to be doing a job that will demand a lot of extra energy, increase your safflower oil intake and you'll have all the energy you need for that extra work. I've found that when I don't take safflower oil capsules with my meals, I seem to have an energy sag, usually in the middle of the morning and the middle of the afternoon. But when I do take them, I'm full of vigor all day long.

Now I'm in my upper fifties and I really put in a long day, too. I don't boast; I'm up at 6:15 or 6:30 every morning and I'm on the go right up to 11 o'clock at night. I take no naps; I have no rest periods; but as long as I take my safflower oil capsules along with my non-glue-food diet, I suffer no loss of energy. My patients find the same thing to be true with them.

"I've experimented with this," Lawrence told me. "I wanted to see if there is any difference. I stopped taking my safflower oil capsules for a week to see what would happen. Well, my energy really sags when I don't take them. I run out of gas in the middle of the morning and in the middle of the afternoon. And at night I fall asleep in the chair watching television.

"There's a definite difference when I don't take my safflower oil capsules. I just don't have as much energy as when I do."

Add multi-vitamin, multi-mineral supplements to your diet

Although I will discuss the functions of vitamins and minerals in complete detail in a later chapter, I want to cover them briefly here since I do consider them to be such an important part of the non-glue-food diet.

When I first opened my office many years ago, I felt a person should be able to obtain all the vitamins and minerals he needed from the foods he ate, especially if he included all the basic foods in his diet, for instance, meat, fruits, vegetables, and so on.

However, as I have watched the continual deterioration of food quality over the years, and as I've read the work of Doctors Pauling and Shute on Vitamins C and E respectively, as well as the reports of many other researchers, I've become convinced that vitamin and mineral supplements are the cheapest and best health insurance that you can possibly buy.

I take vitamin and mineral supplements every day and I urge all my patients to do the same. I would also recommend strongly that you buy a *natural* vitamin-mineral product rather than an artificial or a synthetic one, for there is a difference between natural and synthetic or artificial vitamin and mineral products.

Synthetic vs. natural vitamins

Early in the 20th Century, scientists discovered vitamins as vital nutrients in food. They then found a way to extract these vitamins so they could make them synthetically in a laboratory.

So today, all synthetic vitamins are made by chemically duplicating the molecular structure of the vitamin found in nature. But all you get is that one isolated single synthetic vitamin.

On the other hand, natural vitamins are derived from fresh wholesome food. They come to you along with the extra, naturally associated food factors not found in synthetics. Remember, this is where scientists first discovered vitamins — in food, not in a test tube. Nature invented vitamins. . .scientists did not.

Natural Vitamin C versus synthetic Vitamin C is a good example of the difference between natural and artificial vitamins. In synthetic Vitamin C tablets you get *only* the laboratory-made artificial chemical, ascorbic acid.

But in nature there is much more to Vitamin C than just ascorbic acid. There are all sorts of trace elements, enzyme catalysts, and other nutritional substances that make up the Vitamin C that is found in natural foods. The same can be said for all the other vitamins, especially the vitamin complexes of B and E.

Summary of recommended vitamins and minerals

Here are the vitamins and minerals I take every day and that I recommend my patients take. All the products listed are manufactured by Schiff Natural Food Products of Moonachie, New Jersey, and are specific Schiff trade names. If your health food store does not carry Schiff products, the proprietor can recommend another brand to you.

1. V-Complette Tablets. . .3 tablets daily.
2. Hi-B-Complex. . .2 capsules daily.
3. Vitamin C, 500 mg, Rose Hips. . .2 tablets daily.
4. E-Complex-200. . .4 capsules daily.

The V-Complette Tablets give you a complete multi-vitamin, multi-mineral supplement. They supply you with Vitamins A, B, C, D, and E, as well as such minerals as calcium, phosphorous, iodine, and iron.

You may wonder why I take additional B, C, and E Vitamins, and why I recommend to my patients that they do the same when the V-Complette Tablets already contain them.

Frankly, I believe in taking large amounts of B, C, and E, especially after reading the reports of Dr. Shute in cardiovascular diseases, Dr. Pauling in colds and virus infections, and the statistical reports of other researchers.

So I take additional amounts of these three vitamins and I urge my patients to do the same. For instance, two capsules of the Hi-B-Complex each day give 600 percent of the minimum daily requirement for Vitamins B1 and B2. Two 500 milligram tablets of Vitamin C daily give 16 times the minimum daily requirement, but if you smoke, you will need that extra Vitamin C.

Smoking cigarettes destroys vitamins

Just one cigarette can destroy 25 milligrams of Vitamin C in your body. One package of cigarettes can thus destroy 500 milligrams of Vitamin C or more than eight times your body's minimum daily requirement.

Four capsules of E-Complex-200 give 800 international units of Vitamin E. The minimum daily requirement has not yet been determined for this vitamin, but its need in nutrition is well recognized and firmly established. Vitamin E seems to give the best results when it is taken in large amounts.

I am a strong believer in the maximum dosage of vitamins and minerals for four more reasons. First of all, our foods today are not at all reliable for vitamin and mineral content. Second, the methods of cooking can destroy much of the Vitamins B and C even before we eat the food. Third, vitamins, minerals, and fatty acid supplements are necessary for the production of lean muscle tissue which is replacing the fat you're losing. Fourth, our personal habits — smoking, just for one example — can destroy the vitamin even after it's in the body.

Vitamins B, C, and E are not toxic

Vitamins B, C, and E are not harmful to you and have no bad side effects. Any excess of these three vitamins that is not needed by your body will simply be excreted in the urine. This might seem like a waste to you, but remember that none of these three vitamins can be stored by your body. So it is better to have a little surplus rather than have too little, especially of these three, when you're on a diet.

There have been some instances of Vitamin A poisoning where the vitamin dosage has been *100,000 units or more daily* for many months. Be careful not to exceed 5,000 units daily of Vitamin A.

Also, Vitamin D can prove toxic when *massive doses of 100,000 units a day* are given for several months. Be careful not to exceed 400 units daily for safety.

What to do about parties and drinking

If you will remember, beer, ale, and sweet wines fall into the glue-food category because of their sugar content. Therefore, they are not permitted on your list of alcoholic beverages.

However, this restriction does not apply to such hard liquors as bourbon, Scotch, rye, gin, and vodka.

But you do need to watch what you use for a mix. Regular soft drinks such as cola, ginger ale, and so on are classified as glue-foods because of the sugar they contain. If you use any of these soft drinks for a mix, be sure to buy the ones that are sugar-free. Just read the label so you'll know.

Or, you can use club soda for a mix. It is not a glue-food because it has no sugar. So you can have a whiskey and soda or a Scotch and soda and not violate any of the rules of the non-glue-food diet. You could also mix your bourbon or your Scotch with water. Maybe you can even drink it neat and use the water for a chaser.

A martini or two is also permissible for the gin is not a glue-food. Neither is vodka, if you prefer a vodka martini. The dry vermouth is, but it is a very minor glue-food for it contains so little sugar, and if you make your martini very, very dry, so much the better. Sweet vermouth is a different story altogether. It has 12 times as much sugar as dry vermouth.

The big villain at a party is not a Scotch and soda, a bourbon and soda, or your dry martini, but the beer, ale, sweet wines, and *the glue-foods you eat while you drink.*

But you can still snack and not feel you're being left out by not eating anything. All you need do is stick to the tidbits that have a high protein value. You can eat all you want of such items as cheese, bacon bits, chicken livers, shrimp, sardines, ham, beef, and the like.

Snacks to avoid

But stay away completely from such glue-foods as cheese spread on *bread* or tiny *crackers. It isn't the cheese that does* the damage; it's the bread and the crackers. The same can be said for food fried in batter or bread crumbs. The food itself — French fried shrimp, for instance — is fine, but the batter and bread crumbs it's fried in are not.

And don't go near that bowl of garlic, onion, or blue cheese dip. The dip won't hurt you too much, but the potato chip you use to scoop it up with is one of the most potent glue-foods you can ever eat. Again, it isn't that one potato chip that hurts you, but as the TV commercial says, "Who can eat just one?" And that's the big problem for you — quantity.

Also, it's best to avoid the nuts. A few won't matter, but in that respect, they are just like potatoes or potato chips. No one ever eats just a few nuts — they eat a lot of nuts — handfuls, to be exact. Cashews can melt in your mouth like snow in a hot sun and before you know it, you've consumed far more than you need for immediate energy. So stay away from the nut dish at a party.

If there's any doubt at all in your mind about some of these party foods, look back at the list of glue-foods to avoid, and I'm sure your question will be answered completely and immediately.

However, you can still go to a party and not feel that you're sticking out like a sore thumb. You can still eat and not insult your hostess. And you can still drink and not insult your host. So cheers!

Forget your excess fat problem for 30 days

That's all there is to this first version of the non-glue-food diet: just these few simple rules to follow. You can easily lose all your excess fat in a short time if you'll follow them thoroughly.

One time Carl S. was telling me how he stayed sober on the AA program. "All you have to do is stay sober just one day at a time," Carl said. "You don't have to go the rest of your life without taking a drink. If I had to do that, I'd never make it.

"So I just turn my back on my problem and I forget it for only one day at a time. Before long that one day has stretched into 7, then into 14, and before I know it, I've been sober a whole month without even thinking about my drinking problem. Fact is, Doc, I haven't had a drink for nearly 10 years now, but I did it by staying sober just one day at a time!"

That's what I want you to do, too. Diet just one day at a time. Don't worry about tomorrow; let tomorrow take care of itself. Concentrate your efforts only on today. Follow these few simple rules of the non-glue-food diet, turn your back on your excess fat problem one day at a time for 30 days, and then come back and see me. I know you will have lost from 8 to 12 pounds of your excess fat.

Points to remember

If you have 20 pounds or less of excess fat to lose, then these are the main points you ought to keep in mind:
1. Eliminate all the glue-foods from your diet.
2. Eat all the protein foods you want.
3. Eat all the fresh, frozen, or canned fruits and vegetables you want.
4. Don't eat potatoes, potato chips, or any sort of potato product.
5. Don't eat fresh or frozen vegetables that have been creamed.
6. For even faster results, use the *Three-to-One Rule.*
7. Avoid all fruit that has been canned or frozen in sugar or syrup. Don't eat any dried fruits.
8. Remember the beverages you can and can't drink.
9. Use only the dressings, garnishes, and condiments that are not glue-foods.
10. Establish a sensible eating pattern as soon as possible.
11. Use fresh fruits to satisfy your sweet tooth.
12. To speed up your fat loss and to give you added energy, add polyunsaturated fats to your diet.
13. Add vitamin and mineral supplements to your diet.
14. Watch what you eat and drink at parties.
15. Follow these simple rules and forget all about your excess fat problem for 30 days.

SECTION II: How to lose four or five pounds each week

No matter how much you weigh, you would eventually get rid of all your excess fat by following the original non-glue-food diet I just gave you in Section I because the only way to lose your excess fat is to stop eating glue-foods. They are the cause of your problem. And if you were to do only that, over a period of time you'd get rid of all your excess fat.

However, if you have from 20 to 40 pounds of excess fat to lose, or perhaps even more than that, two problems come up at once that must be taken into consideration. The first one is your American impatience; the second one is the physical condition of your pancreas.

Americans are the most impatient people on this earth. They always want everything done yesterday, if not sooner. It has probably taken you from 5 to 15 years or more to put on all your excess fat, but I know that you want it all off by tomorrow.

And that's why the original non-glue-food diet in Section I will not work fast enough for you if you have more than 20 pounds of excess fat to lose. Sure it'll take it all off you in time, if you'll just give it the proper time. But since chances are that you won't, I've come up with this speeded-up version of the non-glue-food diet that you can use.

Then there's also your pancreas to consider. You see, your pancreas is so trigger-happy from the glue-foods you've been eating that it reacts at once to produce insulin when almost any amount of either man-made or natural carbohydrate enters your blood stream. And when your pancreas produces insulin, your excess blood sugar is always converted into permanent body fat.

Your pancreas will now treat some fruits and vegetables as glue-foods

Although fruits and vegetables are not actually glue-foods, your pancreas now reacts to some of them as if they were. In other words, your pancreas is now so sensitive that it treats the natural carbohydrates in starchy fruits and vegetables as if they were all man-made carbohydrates, or glue-foods.

This means, then, that until your pancreas becomes

desensitized, you'll have to avoid certain fruits and vegetables. You won't have to avoid all of them, just the ones that are highest in natural carbohydrates. After your pancreas returns to its normal function, you can then return to eating all the fruits and vegetables you want, no matter what kind.

However, you'll never be able to return to eating *all* the glue-foods that caused your problem in the first place, primarily the ones that contain sugar, flour, and cornstarch. But by that time you'll be feeling so much better and enjoying the benefits so much of being slim and trim and healthy that you won't want to eat any fattening glue-foods at all.

"You couldn't pay me enough money to get me off the non-glue-food diet if I had to go back to what I was like before," Bob told me. "I've lost 53 pounds on your non-glue-food diet and I feel 10 years younger, Doc. I can work all day and never feel tired. No sir, you couldn't sell me on eating glue-foods again. Not ever."

The non-glue-food diet in Part 1 of this Section is just right for you

If you have more than 20 pounds of excess fat to lose, or if you're in an especially big hurry to lose whatever extra pounds you are carrying around, then the non-glue-food diet in Part 1 of this section is just the thing for you.

However, if you have more than 40 pounds to lose, you'll need to follow the additional instructions that are given in Part 2.

I would also like to point out here that once in a while patients of mine who have less than 20 pounds of excess fat to lose are not able to get rid of all of it on the non-glue-food diet in Section I. Because of some peculiar quirk in their basic fat metabolism, or because their pancreas is so sensitive to all carbohydrates — both natural and man-made — they have to use the non-glue-food diet in Part 1 of this section to get the full results they want.

If that should happen to you, don't get upset and fret about it. No two human bodies are exactly alike nor do any two people respond to treatment in precisely the same way. All of us are different from each other.

But it shouldn't really matter to you which version of the non-glue-food diet you use to get the results you want. Getting rid of your excess fat so you can enjoy the benefits of being slim and trim is what really counts — not the method you use to get there. One of these versions will do the trick for you.

PART 1

If you have between 20 and 40 pounds of excess fat to lose, the non-glue-food diet here in Part 1 is the one you should use. All you need do is follow the easy rules from Section I that I've listed below plus the additional rules I'll give you in a few moments.

Follow these basic rules from Section I

1. Eliminate all the glue-foods from your diet. Refer to page 72.
2. Eat all the protein foods you want. See page 73.
3. Drink all you want of these beverages. Turn to page 80.
4. Avoid or limit these beverages. See page 81.
5. Use these dressings and garnishes freely. See page 82.
6. You can use these condiments for seasoning. Turn to page 82 .
7. Establish a sensible eating pattern as soon as possible. Refer to page 83 .
8. To speed up your fat loss and to give you extra energy, add polyunsaturated fats to your diet. See page 86 .
9. Add multi-vitamin, multi-mineral supplements to your diet. Turn to page 90 .
10. Stick to the non-glue-foods when you party. Refer to page 93 .
11. Forget your excess fat problem for 30 days.

The two main rules that are deleted from the previous section

since they do *not* apply to you here are these:
1. Eat all the fresh, frozen, or canned fruits and vegetables that you want.
2. How to satisfy your sweet tooth.

The remainder of Part 1 of this section will be used to give you the new rules that take the place of these two.

Use these additional rules to speed up your excess fat loss to four or five pounds each week

This second version of the original non-glue-food diet grew out of the *Three-to-One Rule*. If you will remember, leafy vegetables have more cellulose and fiber than the seed or kernel types of vegetables. Therefore, the leafy ones have much less natural carbohydrate than the seed type have.

The diet in this part accomplishes two things for you. First of all, it helps you get rid of your excess fat even faster, and that's what it's all about. Second, it helps you desensitize your pancreas more rapidly by reducing even further your natural carbohydrate intake. You accomplish this by using some discretion in your choice of the fresh fruits and vegetables that you eat. In other words, the main change in Part 1 is the limitation of the fruits and vegetables that you can eat.

Limit your vegetable purchases to about 40¢ each day

To psychologically help my fat patients who have more than 20 pounds of excess fat to lose, I've made up a kind of shopping game they can play. Here's how it works:

I furnish you with a list of vegetables you can "buy" at the market place or the grocery store. Unless the vegetable is on my list, you can't buy it. Of course, if you can't buy it, then you can't possibly eat it.

However, don't be concerned. The list of vegetables you can buy to eat is long and varied. Your vegetables cost you from 5 cents to 12 cents a cup. You can spend up to 40 cents a day.

No credit is allowed, nor are you permitted to save up by spending 30 cents one day and 50 cents the next. Forty cents each day is it. If you are a smart shopper, though, you'll get more for your money.

The vegetables available to you at the market place are shown on the following list with their average cost per cup. "Prices" are based on Home and Garden Bulletin No. 72, *Nutritive Value of Foods,* published by the United States Department of Agriculture,   wherever possible. It will also give you an idea of relative costs of the various foods listed.

Vegetable	*Cost per Cup*
Asparagus, fresh	5¢
Asparagus, canned	7¢
Bamboo shoots	7¢
Bean sprouts, mung	5¢
Bean sprouts, soy	4¢
Beans, snap green, fresh	7¢
Beans, snap green, canned	10¢
Beans, snap, yellow or wax, fresh	6¢
Beans, snap, yellow or wax, canned	9¢
Beet greens	5¢
Broccoli	7¢
Brussels sprouts	10¢
Cabbage, raw, shredded	4¢
Cabbage, cooked	6¢
Cabbage, Chinese, raw	2¢
Cabbage, Chinese, cooked	4¢
Cauliflower	5¢
Celery, raw	2¢
Celery, cooked	4¢
Chard, leaves and stalks	6½¢
Collards	9¢
Dandelion greens	12¢
Eggplant	8¢
Endive, raw	½¢

Escarole, raw	½¢
Kale	4¢
Kohlrabi	8¢
Lettuce	2¢
Mushrooms, canned	6¢
Mustard greens	6¢
Okra	6¢
Sauerkraut	7¢
Spinach	6¢
Squash, *summer*	7¢
Squash, zucchini	6¢
Tomatoes, canned	10¢
Tomatoes, fresh	9¢
Tomato juice	10¢
Turnips	8¢
Turnip greens	5¢

As you can see from this, you do have a large shopping list to choose from. Generally speaking, your best buys will be the more leafy vegetables. They tend to fill and satisfy because of their cellulose and fiber. They are also the *cheapest* ones to buy.

Some vegetables are almost free of charge. For instance, green onions, green peppers, radishes, and cucumbers used in your salads are priced so low that you need not even figure their cost. That's why they're not even included on this list.

Other than those free vegetables I just mentioned for your salads, *do not eat any vegetables that are not on this list.* They are far too expensive for you if you want to speed up your excess fat loss to four or five pounds each week.

Just for example, baked beans can run as high as 53¢ a cup. Other beans, such as lima, navy, pinto, and kidney also cost far too much for you to consider buying them.

So does corn: it runs from 38¢ to more than 50¢ a cup. Black-eyed peas are 29¢; green peas 31¢. Winter squash will cost you at least 32¢. Potatoes are out of sight, especially the candied sweet ones at 60¢ a cup.

When you're down to your ideal weight, you can consider eating some of the more expensive vegetables. But until you do lose all your excess fat, please don't waste your money on them.

Denita's Experience

"This shopping list idea has really helped me," Denita said. "Instead of having to weigh or measure my food, I can tell at a glance what I'm entitled to eat and I can plan my meals easily. Dieting can be a lot more fun when you don't have to use the food scales. Of course, the real fun comes when you actually lose weight. This is the first time that's ever happened to me and I've tried a lot of other diets before."

Denita's case is quite spectacular. She's lost more than 70 pounds in a little over a year and has dropped from 210 down to 138. She was only 10 pounds away from her final goal — 128 pounds — and she made it in good time.

Limit your fresh fruits to no more than 30¢
each day

Fresh fruits are even more expensive for you to buy than vegetables. Most of them are not measured in cups as vegetables are. However, the size of your purchase as well as the price is indicated on your shopping list. So it is extremely easy for you to figure out the cost of a day's shopping. Best buys are marked by an asterisk.

No dried fruits are included on this list nor are any fruits that have been canned in sugar or syrup. These are glue-foods and are not permitted. Besides, the cost of them is completely beyond reason. You can substitute fruits canned in water for the fresh ones if you prefer to do so.

Do not eat any fruits that are not on this list. Do not eat more than you are permitted to eat. The limit is 30 cents a day.

FRUIT	SERVING	COST
Applesauce, *unsweetened*	1/2 cup	13¢
Apricots, raw*	3 medium	14¢
Avocado, *California*	1	13¢
Blackberries, raw*	1 cup	19¢
Blueberries, raw	1 cup	21¢
Cantaloupe	1/2 medium	14¢
Cherries, fresh, pitted*	1 cup	20¢
Grapefruit*	1/2	12¢
Grapefruit juice	1/2 cup	12¢
Honeydew melon*	1 medium wedge	8¢
Mango, raw	1/2 medium	17¢
Nectarine	1 small	17¢
Papaya*	1 cup	18¢
Peach, raw	1	10¢
Pear, raw,	1/2	13¢
Pineapple, raw, diced, unsweetened	1 cup	19¢
Plum	1	7¢
Raspberries, red*	1 cup	17¢
Strawberries*	1 cup	13¢
Tangerine	1	10¢

How to satisfy your sweet tooth

The best way to satisfy your sweet tooth on this version of the non-glue-food diet is by eating the best buys in fruit, such as strawberries, red raspberries, cherries, etc. Of those three, strawberries cost the least and contain the most Vitamin C.

Now at first glance, it would seem that the subheading back in Section I, *How to Satisfy Your Sweet Tooth,* is the same as this one since both use fruits to do that.

However, there is a marked difference. In Section I, you had no limit whatever placed on you as to the amount or the type of fresh fruit you could eat. But here, you have certain definite limitations, not only to the kind of fruit you can eat, but also, as to the amount.

PART 2

This version of the non-glue-food diet is for those who have more than 40 pounds to lose; or for those who want to lose all their excess fat as rapidly as possible; or for those whose carbohydrate metabolism is so far out of whack it will not respond satisfactorily to either of the first two versions of the non-glue-food diet.

There are *three major changes* you must make from the non-glue-food diet that I just gave you in Part 1 of this same section. They are:

1. Eliminate all fruit from your diet.
2. A new way to satisfy your sweet tooth.
3. What to do about alcohol.

Eliminate all fruit from your diet

You must eliminate all the fruit from your diet *except the juice of one lemon or one lime daily.* Don't worry, you're not going to develop a Vitamin C deficiency as long as you take the juice of one lemon or one lime each day. Besides, you'll get all the ascorbic acid you need if you take the Vitamin C supplement I recommended to you back in Section I.

Aside from the glue-foods, fruit is the greatest stimulator of the pancreas because of the high natural sugar content. That's why you have to eliminate it from your diet if you have more than 40 pounds to lose.

Here's a new way to satisfy your sweet tooth

This gets tough to do when you can't eat any fresh fruit. However, a little ingenuity can still turn the trick for you.

You can make some *gelatin* desserts with artificial sweeteners. Be sure that you use gelatin such as that manufactured by the Knox Gelatin people of Johnstown, New York, or the D-Zerta brand of gelatin desserts made by the General Foods Corporation of White Plains, New York.

If you use the Knox Gelatin, you'll need to add an artificial flavor and sweetener. If you use the D-Zerta brand gelatin, you'll not need to add anything at all for it already has artificial flavor and sweetening in it.

I do not advise using Jello or similar dessert types instead of gelatin. They are not the same as gelatin at all. The biggest ingredient of Jello and similar types is sugar, one of your biggest enemies on the non-glue-food diet. Take a look at the label and you'll see what I mean.

What to do about alcohol

I've saved the bad news in this part until last. As you well know, up to now you've been lucky in this department. But if you have more than 40 pounds of excess fat to lose, you should eliminate not only beer, ale, and sweet wines from your diet, but also, the hard stuff you were allowed before.

Although alcohol is not a true carbohydrate, it does act like one in your body. It makes your pancreas discharge insulin just as a glue-food does, even though there's no excess sugar in your blood stream. And when insulin is discharged, your pituitary gland stops manufacturing the fat metabolizing hormone that helps burn up the excess fat in your body.

When you have more than 40 pounds of excess fat to get rid of, well, you simply can't afford to let that happen. Therefore, it's extremely important that you eliminate all alcoholic beverages from your diet during the first 30 days.

After that, you can add it sparingly. For instance, one or two martinis before dinner ought to be enough.

PART 3

The non-glue-food diet in Part 3 should be used only as a last resort when all else fails. Not that it's dangerous — it isn't. But it can become monotonous. I call it the *Eskimo Diet* or the *Caveman's Diet.*

You see, about 5 out of every 100 of my fat patients have to use this version of the non-glue-food diet to get rid of their excess fat because their pancreas is so sensitive it discharges insulin at the slightest provocation. Even the slightest hint of carbohydrate, natural or man-made, in the diet triggers their pancreas.

So they have no choice but to resort to this last version of my non-glue-food diet which has absolutely no carbohydrate of any sort. It contains only protein and fat. But as you have already found out, diets of protein and fat without any carbohydrate at all are not dangerous in any way.

Remember the remarks of Dr. Bondy who said, "No carbohydrate is necessary in the diet. It has been shown by experiments time and again that man can live in good health for month after month on a diet of meats and fats."

That a human being can get along well without carbohydrates was also proven by Viljalmur Stefansson and Dr. Anderson during their winters in the Canadian Arctic on a diet of meat and fat.

Then there were also the successful diet experiments of Doctors DuBois, Donaldson, Pennington, and Gehrmann, all of which proved beyond a doubt that people can get rid of their excess fat on a diet consisting only of meat and fat and still remain in excellent health.

So you see, there's nothing at all for you to worry about if you do have to resort to this version of the non-glue-food diet. You must be sure, however, to take vitamin and mineral supplements. That is no longer just a recommendation; now consider it a must.

Patients of mine who've had to use this version of the non-glue-food diet often use the following procedure: They will go on the Eskimo Diet for one week. Then they'll switch to the diet in Section II, Part 2 — the diet just before this one — for one week. Then they'll come back to the Eskimo Diet again.

By switching back and forth every other week this way, their diet does not get too monotonous for them; they are able to get rid of their excess fat, and that's what really counts.

Rather than list the foods you cannot eat, it is much simpler for me to list the foods you are permitted to have and the few rules you must follow. It'll take much less time and space that way.

1. You may eat meat of any sort – beef, pork, ham, bacon, lamb, etc. – preferably cooked in polyunsaturated fats.
2. You may eat poultry of all kinds, skin and all – chicken, turkey, duck – also preferably cooked in polyunsaturated fats.
3. You may also have seafood or fish of any kind. Tuna, salmon, and sardines packed in oil are excellent. Lobster with melted butter is permitted, so is shrimp. Any kind of fish can be eaten. You can cook it any way you desire, but frying it in polyunsaturated fat is best.
4. Eggs may be eaten. You may cook them any way you want.
5. Cheeses such as Cheddar, Swiss, Edam, American, etc. are permitted.
6. You may use such common seasonings as salt and pepper.
7. Drink as much water, tea, diet cola, club soda, and other sugar-free soft drinks as you want. Limit your coffee to no more than one or two cups with breakfast.
8. You should take from one to three safflower oil capsules with each meal – breakfast, dinner, and supper. You should also take a multi-vitamin multi-mineral supplement daily.
9. Eat all you want of these foods; there is no limit.
10. Nothing else is permitted on this version of the non-glue-food diet. If you don't see it listed here, don't eat it or drink it.

SECTION III: Here's a quick summary of the non-glue-food diets in Chapter Three

I know that I've covered a tremendous amount of material

here in Chapter Three, so in this section I'd like to cover briefly the main points you ought to remember about each version of the non-glue-food diet. That way, you'll have them all in one place for quick and ready reference.

As I'm sure you realize by now, these four versions of the non-glue-food diet differ from one another primarily in the amount of natural carbohydrate that is allowed in each one. The more sensitive your pancreas is, the less carbohydrate it will tolerate and the stricter your diet will be.

The original non-glue-food diet has lots of natural carbohydrate in it for those who have only 20 pounds or less of excess fat to lose. For those who have between 20 and 40 pounds to get rid of, the natural carbohydrate intake is sharply reduced. For those with more than 40 pounds to lose, the natural carbohydrate content is cut even further, while for the really hard shell cases, it is eliminated altogether.

If you have 20 pounds or less of excess fat to lose, here are the main points you ought to remember:

1. Eliminate all the glue-foods from your diet.
2. Eat all the protein foods you want.
3. Eat all the fresh, frozen, or canned fruits and vegetables you want.
4. Don't eat potatoes, potato chips, or any sort of potato products.
5. Don't eat any fresh or frozen vegetables that have been creamed.
6. For even faster results, use the *Three-to-One Rule* (page 79).
7. Avoid all fruit that has been canned or frozen in sugar or syrup. Don't eat any dried fruits.
8. Drink only sugar-free beverages.
9. Use only the dressings, garnishes, and condiments that are not glue-foods.
10. Establish a sensible eating pattern as soon as possible.
11. Use fresh fruits to satisfy your sweet tooth.
12. To speed up your fat loss and give you added energy, add polyunsaturated fats to your diet.

13. Add vitamin and mineral supplements to your diet.
14. Watch what you eat and drink at parties.
15. Follow these simple rules and forget all about your fat problem for 30 days.

If you have from 20 to 40 pounds of excess fat to get rid of, these basic rules of the original non-glue-food diet still apply, but you must limit your fruit and vegetable intake as indicated in Part 1 of Section II to cut down on the natural carbohydrates in your diet. This is the major difference in the second version.

If you have more than 40 pounds to lose, your natural carbohydrate intake must be reduced even further. No fruit at all is allowed except for the juice of one lemon or one lime daily. No alcoholic beverages are permitted. You must satisfy your sweet tooth only with artificially sweetened gelatin.

If you're really a hard case, you'll need to go to the *Eskimo Diet* or the *Caveman's Diet* — meat, poultry, fish, seafood, eggs, cheese, and fats — until you get your pancreas desensitized. After you've lost 10 to 15 pounds on this version, you can switch to one of the other versions to check your pancreas out. If you start to gain weight again, you know that your pancreas is still too sensitive to tolerate carbohydrate, so come back immediately to this diet. Sooner or later, it will become desensitized. Just give it time.

SECTION IV: A Bit of Advice Before You Start Your Diet

Now before you actually start on your non-glue-food diet to gain the benefits of being slim and trim, I'd like to answer any questions you might have on your mind.

Just for instance, you might be concerned about eating eggs and your blood cholesterol level. This is a question a new patient of mine will sometimes bring up.

First of all, if you happen to be allergic to eggs, don't eat any. Although I consider them to be one of the finest all-around complete foods available, they're not absolutely necessary to your diet. Besides, my non-glue-food diet shows you what you can eat — not what you must eat. I'm not forcing you to eat anything.

But if you do know your cholesterol count is high, and if you're concerned about it, then limit the number of eggs you eat each week. I want you to be able to start on your non-glue-food diet without any misgivings and with complete confidence. I don't want you to have any doubts in your mind at all about what the non-glue-food diet will do for you.

Various studies have shown that even when a person is taking in 800 milligrams of cholesterol each day on a diet that is high in animal fat, his liver will still manufacture as much as 3,000 milligrams per day. You see, three-fourths of your body's cholesterol comes from what your body manufactures itself.

Not only that, there is an internal mechanism to control the amount of cholesterol in your body. The more cholesterol you eat, the less your body is required to make; the less cholesterol you take in, the more your body is required to make.

Now let's move on to the problem of high blood pressure and heart disease. Many times my fat patients do have excessively high blood pressure and an overloaded heart when they first come to me. So they want to know if the non-glue-food diet could put a strain on their heart and their blood pressure due to the change in food intake.

Well, let me tell you quickly that I know of nothing that will help take the strain off your cardiovascular system faster than your loss of weight on the non-glue-food diet. There is absolutely no doubt in my mind that when you get rid of your excess fat, you will lengthen your life expectancy. Studies made by many insurance companies have proven that any number of times.

If you have diabetes and are already taking insulin, you should not go on the non-glue-food diet, or any other diet for that matter, without consulting with your own physician first. Or if you have any condition that has caused your doctor to put you on a diet, you would be wise to check with him first before changing it.

In fact, you would be sensible to check with your own doctor if you have any ailment of any sort before you begin your diet. I know the non-glue-food diet cannot hurt you, but I'd like you to know that, too.

Only about 5 out of every 100 people have some sort of metabolic disturbance that keeps them from getting rid of their excess fat on a *proper* reducing diet. If you happen to be one of those rare 1-out-of-20 persons, your doctor no doubt has already told you so. But if you're not, the non-glue-food diet will help you get rid of your excess fat.

What to do when you eat out

I am fortunate enough to have my choice of four excellent cafeterias all within easy driving distance of both my office and my home. When I eat out, most of the time I prefer a cafeteria for I don't have to worry about substitutions. I can pick and choose as I please from the various items on the serving line.

In the beginning, it could be a bit tough for you to get past all the potatoes, the pies, the cakes, and all the fancy desserts. But before too long, you'll lose your yen for all these fattening glue-foods. That's one of the delightful dividends of the non-glue-food diet — losing your craving for man-made carbohydrates, the sweets and starches.

I normally take meat of some kind, a tossed green salad with oil and vinegar or Roquefort dressing, and two green vegetables. To tell the truth, I'm just as full — in fact, I'm more satisfied — than when I used to get a salad, meat, potatoes, and gravy, two or three vegetables, three slices of bread, and pumpkin pie with whipped cream.

Non-glue-foods are much more filling and satisfying than glue-foods, as you'll soon find out. They stick to your ribs and make your hunger stay away much longer than do the glue-foods. My wife, who has no weight problem at all as I have, eats exactly the same things that I do. She avoids glue-foods completely and she says she feels a thousand percent better than she used to feel.

I know one thing for sure. Non-glue-foods must be good for

her for she doesn't begin to show her age. We have three grown children and several grandchildren now, yet I've had people ask me if she was my second wife for she looks so much younger than she actually is. But aside from eating non-glue-foods and avoiding all the man-made carbohydrates, she makes no effort at all to combat her age.

How to handle an obnoxious waiter

Although we usually eat in a cafeteria when we eat out, there are times when we prefer a restaurant with white linen and candlelight, especially when it's a night out on the town.

As far as I'm concerned, if you go to a restaurant where a waiter gives you static about substitutions, I think the best solution is simply to go somewhere else.

However, if you insist on staying there, you'll find his attitude changes immediately when some money is placed in his hand. When all other human motives fail, you can always depend on greed.

If you don't care to go either of these two routes, then simply put your foot down and insist on substituting a green vegetable for your potatoes or whatever else it is you want. Tell him you have a terrible allergy to potatoes (and you have — they make you fat) that makes you deathly sick and that you react to them immediately. Take it from me, that always works.

My father-in-law, who ran an extremely successful restaurant for more than 25 years, always told me the one thing he feared most of all was the possibility of food poisoning or someone getting sick in his place. He is not alone. It's the one thing every restaurant owner dreads above everything else.

Of course, it would help if you could schedule your meals before or after the rush hours when you eat out during the day if you eat in a restaurant instead of a cafeteria. For instance, you could eat your lunch early or late instead of going between 12:00 and 1:00 when everyone else goes. Your waiter won't be rushed then and chances are, you'll encounter no problems with him at all.

Don't complicate your diet; keep it simple

In the next chapter I'll give you my non-glue-food diet meal-planning *guide*. I emphasize the word "guide," for that's exactly what it is — a guide. You see, I frankly feel the more complicated a diet becomes, the more likely a person is not to follow it. So I've kept my non-glue-food diet meal-planning guide as simple as possible.

To show you how simple, yet nourishing, the non-glue-food diet can be, I'd like to tell you what my own normal daily intake is.

Let's start with breakfast. When you do away with all the glue-foods, breakfast becomes a very simple matter: bacon, ham, breakfast steak, or pork chops, and eggs. I scramble my eggs, make a cheese omelet, fry them hard, over-easy, sunny-side up, soft boiled, poached, or any other way I can think of for variety. I've been eating that kind of breakfast for a good many years now, and I still enjoy it.

I usually eat two green salads a day, one of these at lunch time. I use primarily lettuce, tomatoes, green peppers, green onions, and radishes. To this I add either tuna, shrimp, salmon, boned turkey or chicken, ham, or beef. I throw in some chunks of Cheddar cheese and then to top it all off with blue cheese or Roquefort dressing. And that's my normal lunch.

You can use a variety of vegetables, too, to make your own green salads: cabbage (regular or Chinese), celery, chicory, chives, cucumbers, endive, escarole, lettuce, olives, green onions, dill or sour pickles, parsley, green peppers, radishes, scallions, watercress.

And that's only the base. You can really spice it up with tuna, shrimp, chicken, ham, beef, etc., and salad dressing (oil and vinegar, Roquefort, blue cheese), just as I do.

For supper or dinner — whatever you call it where you live — I eat meat of some sort — steak, roast beef, chicken, fish, etc. — another small salad without all the extra trimmings except for salad dressing, and one or two green vegetables.

So you see, I don't use a lot of complicated and fancy menu

planning. I keep it plain and simple; it's much easier that way.

Besides, once you become glue-food conscious, you'll have no difficulty whatever in adjusting your own favorite recipes to make them free of the man-made carbohydrates. Before long you'll develop a brand new set of tastes for the high protein foods that furnish energy without putting on extra pounds of excess fat.

Admittedly, the hardest foods to replace in the non-glue-food diet will be bread, potatoes, pasta, and baked goods. But it will be well worth the effort you put out when you see your pounds and inches melting away and you start feeling full of vigor and vitality again.

Now if you're ready, let's get right on to the next chapter so I can tell you all about your

NON-GLUE-FOOD DIET MEAL-PLANNING GUIDE

4. Your non-glue-food meal-planning guide

I have divided this chapter into five sections for your convenience. Section I gives you your basic meal-planning guide if you have 20 pounds or less of excess fat to lose; Section II is for those who have from 20 to 40 pounds to get rid of; Section III gives the meal-planning guide for those with over 40 pounds of excess fat, while Section IV is for the really hard-shell case. Section V contains some non-glue-food recipes that are favorites of mine; I'm sure you'll like them, too.

Before I leave this short introduction, I want to say that the basic meal-planning guide is essentially the same in each section throughout the chapter. That is to say, it is based on the principle of eliminating or avoiding the glue-foods that cause your excess fat. The main differences you'll find between sections lie in the amount of fruits and vegetables you can eat and the variety that is offered.

Just for example, if you have 20 pounds or less of excess fat to lose, I have placed no limit on the variety or the amount of fresh fruits and vegetables you can eat. However, if you have from 20 to 40 pounds to get rid of, you'll find your intake of fruits and vegetables is more limited.

And if you have more than 40 pounds to lose, your fruit intake will be practically eliminated. If you're really a hard-shell case, you'll have to limit yourself primarily to eggs, meat, cheese, poultry, fish and seafood for a while, at least until you start losing some of your excess fat.

You'll find no limit has been placed on the amount of protein or fat you can eat on any version of the non-glue-food diet. However, if you're concerned with your intake of cholesterol, you should cut down as much as possible on the saturated animal fats and increase your intake of polyunsaturated fats.

In Chapter 3, I asked you to add polyunsaturated fats to your diet to speed up your fat loss. You can also cut down on your intake of saturated animal fats by trimming all the visible fat from your meat, by using margarine instead of butter, and by using vegetable oils in your cooking instead of lard and animal shortenings. This will help control your intake of cholesterol.

Again, let me quickly point out to you that your non-glue-food meal-planning guide shows what you can eat, not what you must eat. However, do not cut down on your intake of non-glue-foods, thinking to speed up your fat loss. Remember that non-glue-foods do not cause your excess fat. Glue-foods are solely responsible.

SECTION I: Here's your basic meal-planning guide if you have 20 pounds or less to lose

You will no doubt notice at once that in the non-glue-food meal-planning guides that follow I have placed no limit on the amount or the variety of foods you can eat.

For instance, you may eat as many vegetables as you want with your lunch or dinner. If only one vegetable is shown and you would like to eat two, then do so. Or if it says asparagus and you don't like asparagus, eat another vegetable instead.

Nor have I placed any limit on the size of your meat portions. You can also switch them around freely, too. If it says lamb and you don't like lamb, then substitute beef, pork, hamburger, chicken, or whatever you do like.

The size of your tossed green salads is also up to you. You may use a dressing such as oil and vinegar, Caesar or Roquefort on your salads. I've also included a homemade French dressing in the recipe section I'm sure you'll like. I use it a great deal of the time, adding chunks of blue cheese to spice it up.

Please understand that your daily meal-planning guide is meant to be just that — a guide, not an inflexible iron-clad rule. But I do ask you to avoid the man-made carbohydrates — the glue-foods. That should be easy to do when you have no limit placed on the non-glue-foods that you can eat.

MEAL-PLANNING GUIDE 1

BREAKFAST	Grapefruit juice Bacon Scrambled eggs Coffee or tea
SNACK	High protein food (may consist of meat, seafood, chicken, cheese, etc.)
LUNCH	Beef or chicken bouillon Tossed green salad with tuna, hard-boiled egg, and Cheddar cheese Asparagus Tea or diet soft drink
SNACK	High protein food (as above)
DINNER	Seafood cocktail Roast beef Brussels sprouts Zucchini squash Tossed green salad

Strawberries
Tea or diet soft drink

SNACK   High protein food

MEAL-PLANNING GUIDE 2

BREAKFAST   Tomato juice
Ham
Fried eggs
Coffee or tea

SNACK   High protein food

LUNCH   Beef or chicken bouillon
Cold sliced beef
Broccoli
Tossed green salad
Tea or diet soft drink

SNACK   High protein food

DINNER   Seafood cocktail
Leg of lamb
Eggplant
Kohlrabi
Tossed green salad
Blackberries
Tea or diet soft drink

SNACK   High protein food

MEAL-PLANNING GUIDE 3

BREAKFAST   Cantaloupe
Sausage patties
Cheese omelet
Coffee or tea

SNACK   High protein food

LUNCH   Seafood cocktail
                    Tossed green salad with boned chicken,
                        hard-boiled egg, and Cheddar cheese
                    Cauliflower
                    Tea or diet soft drink

SNACK   High protein food

DINNER   Beef or chicken bouillon
                    Fish (flounder, turbot, haddock, perch, etc.)
                    Snap green beans
                    Cooked celery
                    Tossed green salad
                    Cherries
                    Tea or diet soft drink

SNACK   High protein food

MEAL-PLANNING GUIDE 4

BREAKFAST   Grapefruit
                    Breakfast steak
                    Poached eggs
                    Coffee or tea

SNACK   High protein food

LUNCH   Beef or chicken bouillon
                    Cheeseburger (no bun)
                    Summer squash
                    Tossed salad
                    Tea or diet soft drink

SNACK   High protein food

DINNER   Seafood cocktail
                    Roast pork
                    Snap green beans
                    Cabbage

Tossed green salad
Raspberries
Tea or diet soft drink

SNACK   High protein food

MEAL-PLANNING GUIDE 5

BREAKFAST   Honeydew melon
Link sausage
Soft boiled eggs
Coffee or tea

SNACK   High protein food

LUNCH   Beef or chicken bouillon
Cold roast pork
Okra
Tossed green salad
Tea or diet soft drink

SNACK   High protein food

DINNER   Seafood cocktail
Steak
Yellow wax beans
Asparagus
Tossed green salad
Blueberries
Tea or diet soft drink

SNACK   High protein food

MEAL-PLANNING GUIDE 6

BREAKFAST   Grapefruit juice
Canadian bacon
Baked eggs (baked in casserole on top of
    Canadian bacon)

	Coffee or tea
SNACK	High protein food
LUNCH	Beef or chicken bouillon Tossed green salad with salmon, hard-boiled egg, and Cheddar cheese Kale Tea or diet soft drink
SNACK	High protein food
DINNER	Seafood cocktail Fried chicken Collards Turnips Tossed green salad Peaches Tea or diet soft drink
SNACK	High protein food

MEAL-PLANNING GUIDE 7

BREAKFAST	Tomato juice Bacon Scrambled eggs Coffee or tea
SNACK	High protein food
LUNCH	Beef or chicken bouillon Cold fried chicken Broccoli Tossed green salad Tea or diet soft drink
SNACK	High protein food
DINNER	Seafood cocktail Lamb chops

　　　　　　　　　　Spinach
　　　　　　　　　　Brussels sprouts
　　　　　　　　　　Tossed green salad
　　　　　　　　　　Pineapple, raw, diced, unsweetened
　　　　　　　　　　Tea or diet soft drink

SNACK   High protein food

If you do not lose your excess fat as fast as you think you should on this first version of the non-glue-food diet (2 to 3 pounds each week) you can switch over to the non-glue-food meal-planning guides in Section II.

In my own practice I have found that some patients who have 20 pounds or less of excess fat to lose, but who do not lose 2 to 3 pounds each week, are just on the verge of gaining more weight when they come into my office.

In other words, their pancreas has become more sensitive to carbohydrate intake, and had they not discovered the non-glue-food diet when they did, they would soon be 30 or 40 or more pounds overweight rather than just 20.

If you find yourself in this situation, or if you already have from 20 to 40 pounds of excess fat to lose, then the meal-planning guides in Section II are just right for you.

SECTION II: Here's Your Basic Meal-Planning Guide if you have from 20 to 40 pounds to lose

The major difference between the meal-planning guides in the previous section and in this one is that in this section you are limited to the amount of fresh fruits and vegetables that you can eat. You are not, however, limited in the amounts of meat, poultry, fish, seafood, and cheese, or the size of your tossed green salads that you can have.

MEAL-PLANNING GUIDE 1

BREAKFAST
2/3 cup grapefruit juice
Bacon
Scrambled eggs
Coffee or tea

SNACK
High protein food (may consist of meat,
seafood, chicken, cheese, etc.)

LUNCH
Beef or chicken bouillon
Tossed green salad with tuna, hard-boiled egg,
and Cheddar cheese
1 cup asparagus
Tea or diet soft drink

SNACK
High protein food (as above)

DINNER
Seafood cocktail
Roast beef
1 cup Brussels sprouts
1 cup zucchini squash
Tossed green salad
1 cup strawberries
Tea or diet soft drink

SNACK
High protein food

MEAL-PLANNING GUIDE 2

BREAKFAST
1 glass tomato juice
Ham
Fried eggs
Coffee or tea

SNACK
High protein food

LUNCH
Beef or chicken bouillon

Cold sliced beef
1 cup broccoli
Tossed green salad
Tea or diet soft drink

SNACK   High protein food

DINNER   Seafood cocktail
Leg of lamb
1 cup eggplant
1 cup kohlrabi
Tossed green salad
1 cup blackberries
Tea or diet soft drink

SNACK   High protein food

MEAL-PLANNING GUIDE 3

BREAKFAST   1/2 medium cantaloupe
Sausage patties
Cheese omelet
Coffee or tea

SNACK   High protein food

LUNCH   Seafood cocktail
Tossed green salad with boned chicken,
      hard-boiled egg, and Cheddar cheese
1 cup cauliflower
Tea or diet soft drink

SNACK   High protein food

DINNER   Beef or chicken bouillon
Fish (flounder, turbot, haddock, perch, etc.)
1 cup snap green beans
1 cup cooked celery
Tossed green salad
1 cup cherries
Tea or diet soft drink

SNACK   High protein food

MEAL-PLANNING GUIDE 4

BREAKFAST   1/2 grapefruit
                    Breakfast steak
                    Poached eggs
                    Coffee or tea

SNACK   High protein food

LUNCH   Beef or chicken bouillon
                    Cheeseburger (no bun)
                    1 cup summer squash
                    Tossed salad
                    Tea or diet soft drink

SNACK   High protein food

DINNER   Seafood cocktail
                    Roast pork
                    1 cup snap green beans
                    1 cup cabbage
                    Tossed green salad
                    1 cup raspberries
                    Tea or diet soft drink

SNACK   High protein food

MEAL-PLANNING GUIDE 5

BREAKFAST   1 medium wedge honeydew melon
                    Link sausage
                    Soft boiled eggs
                    Coffee or tea

SNACK   High protein food

LUNCH   Beef or chicken bouillon

Cold roast pork
1 cup okra
Tossed green salad
Tea or diet soft drink

SNACK   High protein food

DINNER   Seafood cocktail
Steak
1 cup yellow wax beans
1 cup asparagus
Tossed green salad
1 cup blueberries
Tea or diet soft drink

SNACK   High protein food

MEAL-PLANNING GUIDE 6

BREAKFAST   1/2 cup grapefruit juice
Canadian bacon
Baked eggs (baked in casserole on top of
    Canadian bacon)
Coffee or tea

SNACK   High protein food

LUNCH   Beef or chicken bouillon
Tossed green salad with salmon, hard-boiled
    egg, and Cheddar cheese
1 cup kale
Tea or diet soft drink

SNACK   High protein food

DINNER   Seafood cocktail
Fried chicken
1 cup collards
1 cup turnips
Tossed green salad

2 raw peaches
Tea or diet soft drink

SNACK   High protein food

MEAL-PLANNING GUIDE 7

BREAKFAST   1 cup tomato juice
Bacon
Scrambled eggs
Coffee or tea

SNACK   High protein food

LUNCH   Beef or chicken bouillon
Cold fried chicken
1 cup broccoli
Tossed green salad
Tea or diet soft drink

SNACK   High protein food

DINNER   Seafood cocktail
Lamp chops
1 cup spinach
1 cup Brussels sprouts
Tossed green salad
1 cup pineapple, raw, diced, unsweetened
Tea or diet soft drink

SNACK   High protein food

SECTION III: Here's Your Basic Meal-Planning Guide if You Have More Than 40 Pounds to Lose

The major differences between the basic meal-planning guides here and in the previous section are these:

1. All fruit is eliminated from your diet except the juice of one lemon or one lime daily.
2. You must use only *gelatin* desserts with artificial flavoring and artificial sweeteners to satisfy your sweet tooth.

MEAL-PLANNING GUIDE 1

BREAKFAST
Juice of one lemon or one lime
Bacon
Scrambled eggs
Coffee or tea

SNACK
High protein food (may consist of meat, seafood, chicken, cheese, etc.)

LUNCH
Beef or chicken bouillon
Tossed green salad with tuna, hard-boiled egg, and Cheddar cheese
1 cup asparagus
Tea or diet soft drink

SNACK
High protein food (as above)

DINNER
Seafood cocktail
Roast beef
1 cup Brussels sprouts
1 cup zucchini squash
Tossed green salad
Gelatin dessert
Tea or diet soft drink

SNACK
High protein food

MEAL-PLANNING GUIDE 2

BREAKFAST
Juice of one lemon or one lime
Ham
Fried eggs

	Coffee or tea
SNACK	High protein food
LUNCH	Beef or chicken bouillon Cold sliced beef 1 cup broccoli Tossed green salad Tea or diet soft drink
SNACK	High protein food
DINNER	Seafood cocktail Leg of lamb 1 cup eggplant 1 cup kohlrabi Tossed green salad Gelatin dessert Tea or diet soft drink
SNACK	High protein food

MEAL-PLANNING GUIDE 3

BREAKFAST	Juice of one lemon or one lime Sausage patties Cheese omelet Coffee or tea
SNACK	High protein food
LUNCH	Seafood cocktail Tossed green salad with boned chicken, hard-boiled egg, and Cheddar cheese 1 cup cauliflower Tea or diet soft drink
SNACK	High protein food
DINNER	Beef or chicken bouillon Fish (flounder, turbot, haddock, perch, etc.)

1 cup snap green beans
1 cup cooked celery
Tossed green salad
Gelatin dessert
Tea or diet soft drink

SNACK   High protein food

MEAL-PLANNING GUIDE 4

BREAKFAST   Juice of one lemon or one lime
                         Breakfast steak
                         Poached eggs
                         Coffee or tea

SNACK   High protein food

LUNCH   Beef or chicken bouillon
                         Cheeseburger (no bun)
                         1 cup summer squash
                         Tossed salad
                         Tea or diet soft drink

SNACK   High protein food

DINNER   Seafood cocktail
                         Roast pork
                         1 cup snap green beans
                         1 cup cabbage
                         Tossed green salad
                         Gelatin dessert
                         Tea or diet soft drink

SNACK   High protein food

MEAL-PLANNING GUIDE 5

BREAKFAST   Juice of one lemon or one lime
                         Link sausage

Soft-boiled eggs
Coffee or tea

SNACK   High protein food

LUNCH   Beef or chicken bouillon
Cold roast pork
1 cup okra
Tossed green salad
Tea or diet soft drink

SNACK   High protein food

DINNER   Seafood cocktail
Steak
1 cup yellow wax beans
1 cup asparagus
Tossed green salad
Gelatin dessert
Tea or diet soft drink

SNACK   High protein food

MEAL-PLANNING GUIDE 6

BREAKFAST   Juice of one lemon or one lime
Canadian bacon
Baked eggs (baked in casserole on top of
    Canadian bacon)
Coffee or tea

SNACK   High protein food

LUNCH   Beef or chicken bouillon
Tossed green salad with salmon, hard-boiled
    egg, and Cheddar cheese
1 cup kale
Tea or diet soft drink

SNACK   High protein food

DINNER   Seafood cocktail
                Fried chicken
                1 cup collards
                1 cup turnips
                Tossed green salad
                Gelatin dessert
                Tea or diet soft drink

SNACK   High protein food

MEAL-PLANNING GUIDE 7

BREAKFAST   Juice of one lemon or one lime
                Bacon
                Scrambled eggs
                Coffee or tea

SNACK   High protein food

LUNCH   Beef or chicken bouillon
                Cold fried chicken
                1 cup broccoli
                Tossed green salad
                Tea or diet soft drink

SNACK   High protein food

DINNER   Seafood cocktail
                Lamb chops
                1 cup spinach
                1 cup Brussels sprouts
                Tossed green salad
                Gelatin dessert
                Tea or diet soft drink

SNACK   High protein food

SECTION IV: Here's Your Basic Meal-Planning Guide for the Eskimo or Caveman's Diet

If your pancreas is so sensitive to carbohydrate that you cannot get rid of your excess fat by using the meal-planning guide in the previous section, then you have no choice but to use the meal-planning guides for the Eskimo or Caveman's diet.

If you do use this version of the non-glue-food diet, you should be sure to take the vitamin and mineral supplements I previously recommended to you. You will especially need the Viatmin C.

I would also recommend the procedure many of my own patients use. They go on the Eskimo diet for one week. Then they use the diet in Section III for the next week. After that they come back to the Eskimo diet again. By switching back and forth every other week this way, their diet does not get too monotonous for them, and they are able to get rid of their excess fat, even though it does take a little more time to do it with this method.

MEAL-PLANNING GUIDE 1

BREAKFAST
Bacon
Scrambled eggs
Coffee or tea

SNACK
High protein food (may consist of meat, seafood, chicken, cheese, etc.)

LUNCH
Beef or chicken bouillon
Tuna
Hard-boiled eggs
Cheese
Tea or diet soft drink

SNACK
High protein food (as before)

DINNER   Beef or chicken bouillon
                Seafood cocktail
                Roast beef
                Cheese
                Tea or diet soft drink

SNACK   High protein food

MEAL-PLANNING GUIDE 2

BREAKFAST   Ham
                Fried Eggs
                Coffee or tea

SNACK   High protein food

LUNCH   Beef or chicken bouillon
                Cold sliced beef
                Cheese
                Hard-boiled eggs
                Tea or diet soft drink

SNACK   High protein food

DINNER   Beef or chicken bouillon
                Seafood cocktail
                Leg of lamb
                Cheese
                Tea or diet soft drink

SNACK   High protein food

MEAL-PLANNING GUIDE 3

BREAKFAST   Sausage patties
                Cheese omelet
                Coffee or tea

SNACK   High protein food

LUNCH   Beef or chicken bouillon
                     Seafood cocktail
                     Fried chicken
                     Hard-boiled eggs
                     Cheese
                     Tea or diet soft drink

SNACK   High protein food

DINNER   Beef or chicken bouillon
                     Fish(flounder, turbot, haddock, perch, etc.)
                     Cheese
                     Tea or diet soft drink

SNACK   High protein food

MEAL-PLANNING GUIDE 4

BREAKFAST   Breakfast steak
                     Poached eggs
                     Coffee or tea

SNACK   High protein food

LUNCH   Beef or chicken bouillon
                     Cheeseburger (no bun)
                     Hard-boiled eggs
                     Tea or diet soft drink

SNACK   High protein food

DINNER   Beef or chicken bouillon
                     Seafood cocktail
                     Roast pork
                     Cheese
                     Tea or diet soft drink

SNACK   High protein food

MEAL-PLANNING GUIDE 5

BREAKFAST   Link sausage
                 Soft boiled eggs
                 Coffee or tea

SNACK   High protein food

LUNCH   Beef or chicken bouillon
                 Cold roast pork
                 Hard-boiled eggs
                 Cheese
                 Tea or diet soft drink

SNACK   High protein food

DINNER   Beef or chicken bouillon
                 Seafood cocktail
                 Steak
                 Cheese
                 Tea or diet soft drink

SNACK   High protein food

MEAL-PLANNING GUIDE 6

BREAKFAST   Canadian bacon
                 Baked eggs (baked in casserole on top of
                     Canadian bacon)
                 Coffee or tea

SNACK   High protein food

LUNCH   Beef or chicken bouillon
                 Salmon
                 Hard-boiled eggs
                 Cheese
                 Tea or diet soft drink

SNACK	High protein food
DINNER	Beef or chicken bouillon
	Seafood cocktail
	Fried chicken
	Cheese
	Tea or diet soft drink
SNACK	High protein food

MEAL-PLANNING GUIDE 7

BREAKFAST	Bacon
	Scrambled eggs
	Coffee or tea
SNACK	High protein food
LUNCH	Beef or chicken bouillon
	Cold fried chicken
	Hard-boiled eggs
	Cheese
	Tea or diet soft drink
SNACK	High protein food
DINNER	Beef or chicken bouillon
	Seafood cocktail
	Lamb chops
	Cheese
	Tea or diet soft drink
SNACK	High protein food

SECTION V: A selected list of My Favorite Non-Glue-Food Recipes

I have not included a long list of non-glue-food recipes. Instead, I have chosen only a few that are favorites of mine and that I thought you might like to add to your own receipe file.

Besides, if you check your own recipes you'll find in a great many instances, you can change a glue-food recipe into a non-glue-food receipe simply by using a sugar substitute in place of granulated white sugar.

Some sugar substitutes you might find to be quite satisfactory, for example *Sug'r Like* and *Sugar Twin*. Both are used spoon for spoon just like ordinary sugar. You can also get a *Brown Sugar Twin* as well as the regular white kind.

Homemade French dressing

2½ cups sugar substitute (Sugar Twin or similar)
3/4 cup white vinegar
1 teaspoon celery seed
2 tablespoons Worcestershire sauce
1 teaspoon salt
2 tablespoons catsup
1 teaspoon dry mustard
1 pint Mazola or safflower oil
1 teaspoon garlic salt
1 medium size onion finely ground or grated

Mix all ingredients together and refrigerate. Allow several days for dressing to blend before using.

This dressing is one of the best homemade dressings I've ever found. If you feel that 2½ cups of the sugar substitute make the dressing too sweet for you, reduce the amount gradually until you discover just the right taste for you. If 2½ cups make it too sour, do just the opposite, of course.

If you happen to give this recipe to some of your thin friends who can eat glue-foods, tell them to use only 2 cups of honey instead of 2½ as indicated for the sugar substitute.

I like to add chunks of blue cheese or Roquefort cheese to this dressing to give it more body, zest, and spice.

Hawaiian barbecue sauce

2 cups water
1 clove garlic (or to taste if you like garlic)
2 bulbs ginger root
4 cups soy sauce (Kikkoman or similar)
2 cups honey
1/2 teaspoon sesame oil
2 jiggers sherry wine

Mix soy sauce, water, honey, sesame oil, and sherry together in a mixing bowl. Grate the ginger root into the bowl — the finer the better. Cut the garlic bud into small pieces and squeeze through a garlic press in the bowl. Stir all ingredients together well and refrigerate. Allow several days to blend together before using.

I know you will be surprised to find that I have allowed you to use honey in this recipe. There are several reasons for this. First of all, honey is a natural sugar and it does not have the harmful effects on your body that granulated refined white sugar has. Second, I know you won't be using this barbecue sauce every day. Third, you won't use the entire batch at one time. Fourth, the natural sugar of honey, just like alcohol, tends to vaporize in flame or open heat, so that the final effects are negligible, especially when you barbecue your food over charcoal.

This is one of the finest barbecue sauces I have ever used. In fact, I'll go even farther than that. I'll say it's the best I've ever tasted. I picked it up from some Nisei friends of ours on a trip to Hawaii some years back.

I recommend *Kikkoman* soy sauce. You will be sadly disappointed if you use an American-made soy sauce.

Hawaiian barbecue sauce can be used to marinate chicken, pork chops, spare ribs, steak, hamburgers, fish, etc. You can broil, bake, or barbecue your food over a charcoal grill. Barbecuing is by far the most preferable method.

I gave this barbecue sauce recipe to a friend of mine in California several years ago. Last year I dropped by to see him. He lives in Monterey and it was one of its usual wet, foggy, and damp spring days.

Grant was cooking chicken that had been soaked in the barbecue sauce. He was using a small charcoal grill — actually a Japanese hibachi — in spite of the bad weather. But he wasn't barbecuing outside.

Instead, he had the hibachi on top of his electric range in the kitchen. He had the exhaust fan turned on to take the charcoal fumes out of the house. That was the best recommendation I've ever seen for this Hawaiian barbecue sauce.

Chicken Hawaiian style

Marinate disjointed chicken in Hawaiian barbecue sauce for at least four hours (I prefer overnight myself). Then bake in medium oven or barbecue over a charcoal grill. Baste occasionally with the barbecue sauce while the chicken is cooking. If you bake the chicken in an oven, you can leave some of the marinade in the pan and let it simmer while it's baking.

Pork chops (or lamb chops) Hawaiian style

Marinate pork chops or lamb chops in the Hawaiian barbecue sauce at least four hours. I prefer overnight. Then broil in a medium oven or barbecue over a charcoal grill, basting occasionally with the sauce while the chops are cooking. You can also bake the chops in the oven. If you do, place them in a pan with some marinade and let them simmer while cooking.

Spare ribs, steak, or any other cut of meat can be prepared in the same way. Hamburgers are delicious with Hawaiian barbecue sauce. They do not need to be marinated, but can be basted while they are cooking. And what the sauce will do for liver is out of this world! I've seen people who couldn't get the first bite of liver past their lips clean their plate and ask for more.

Fish Hawaiian style

You've never really tasted fish until you eat some that has been marinated in this Hawaiian barbeque sauce.

Marinate the fish fillets or slices for 20 minutes to an hour depending on their size and thickness. Score the skin on a whole fish to allow the marinate to penetrate. Charcoal broil, bake, or broil in your oven — brushing over once or twice with the sauce while the fish is cooking.

Even people who've never liked fish will love this kind and they'll even come back for seconds.

Beginner's Sukiyaki

2 pounds sirloin, machine sliced bacon thin by butcher
4 stalks celery cut diagonally in ½ inch pieces
2 onions, sliced lengthwise
1 bunch green onions, cut in 2 inch lengths including
    green ends
1 cup fresh or canned mushrooms, sliced
½ pound spinach, slightly steamed or precooked
1 can (8½ ounces) bamboo shoots, sliced
1½ cups Hawaiian barbecue sauce

Arrange vegetables and meat on large platter. Set electric skillet at 300 degrees and grease with small amount of cooking oil. Add 1/3 meat and cover with 1/2 barbecue sauce. Then add 2/3 vegetables.

Turn ingredients gently while cooking 5 to 6 minutes. Add another 1/3 meat and cook for one more minute. Place directly into plate or bowl and serve

Occasionally replenish skillet with ingredients and sauce as needed. Recipe will serve 6 people. Chicken sukiyaki can be prepared the same way with boned and sliced chicken.

Green beans with brown butter garlic sauce

1 pound green beans
3 quarts boiling water
4½ teaspoons salt
1/4 cup butter
1 clove garlic, thinly sliced
1/4 cup chopped onion
1/4 teaspoon salt

Trim the ends from the washed and drained green beans. Cut them in half or into 2 inch lengths.

Add 4½ teaspoons of salt to the three quarts of boiling water. Slip beans by handfuls into the water, making sure that the water continues to boil rapidly. Then lower the heat, leave uncovered and let them simmer for 6 to 8 minutes. Do not overcook. The beans should be done *crisp* with a bright green color. Drain immediately. If they are not to be used at once, run cold water over them, drain and dry in paper towels. Place them in a covered bowl until they are ready to use.

Now melt the butter in a small pan over low heat. When it begins to darken and turn pale brown, add the sliced garlic. The butter will foam up. Remove from heat until the foam subsides. The garlic should be pale brown around the edges. Now add the chopped onion and cook until the onion is soft. Add the last ¼ teaspoon of salt.

Pour the butter mixture into a large frying pan. Add the green beans and toss or stir over a low flame until the beans are heated thoroughly.

You can substitute other green vegetables that you like for the green beans for added variety.

These are just a few of my favorite recipes you can use on the non-glue-food diet. I could give you more, but this is not a cookbook as such. Besides, if you will check your own favorite recipes, I know you'll find you can change a glue-food recipe into a non-glue-food recipe in a great many instances simply by using a sugar substitute in place of granulated white sugar.

So now if you're ready, I want to move along to the next chapter where I'll tell you

HOW THE NON-GLUE-FOOD DIET CAN MAKE YOU MORE ATTRACTIVE AND INCREASE YOUR SEXUAL POWERS

5. How the non-glue-food diet can make you more attractive and increase your sexual powers

The average person like you and me has six basic needs — six fundamental desires — things he feels he must have if he is to be happy. If any single one of these needs is not fulfilled, a deep-seated feeling of uneasiness and restlessness fills the person.

One of these basic needs is the need for love and affection. Sexual intercourse is also basically important as an integral part of that love and affection between a man and a woman. A marriage cannot be completely unified, loving, and mutually satisfactory unless the sexual experience between the husband and wife is also completely unified, loving, and mutually satisfactory.

If, for one reason or another, sexual love does not develop properly in a marriage, or if in time it fades away and disappears, one or both of the couple will become restless, dissatisfied, irritable, and highly critical of the other person.

The most recent figures indicate that *sexual problems of one kind or another affect at least half of the married couples in the United States today.* How many of these sexual problems are caused by excess fat I frankly do not know, but I do know from personal experience in my own private practice that fat people do have unsatisfactory sex relationships with their marriage partners. In a great many instances, it is the motivating force that brings the patient to my office to ask for help. In fact,

— — —

Ninety-five percent of my fat patients have a problem with sex

If you are fat, then, the chances are also at least 95 out of 100 that you will have a problem with sex, too; for in fat people, the desire for sex and the sex drive is greatly diminished.

And if your desire for sex is diminished, if you are just not as interested as you used to be in sexual activity and love-making, this can create a serious marital problem especially if your marriage partner is slim, willing, and capable.

The lack of sexual response or the lack of sexual desire on the part of one partner in a marriage can destroy the marital relationship, for there cannot possibly be a satisfactory experience for the other partner. When one person has a sexual problem, the other person has to have a sexual problem, too. There is no such thing as a disinterested partner when there is a sexual maladjustment in marriage.

When you lose weight, your love life will improve

When you get rid of your excess fat on my non-glue-food diet, you'll find that your love life will definitely and quickly improve, just as Gary R. found.

Gary's experience

"My wife used to tell me that making love with me was about like having a Saint Bernard in bed with her," Gary told me. "I literally smothered her, and not with affection either, but with a ton of fat. It was no wonder she used to turn her back on me and pretend to be asleep the minute I got into bed. Can't say I blame her one bit, though.

"And on those rare occasions when we did make love, she'd always want me to hurry up and get it over with. She wanted to get rid of me as soon as possible because I was so darn heavy.

"But since I've been on your non-glue-food diet, Doc, things sure have changed for the better. Now she doesn't want me to leave. She holds on to me for as long as she can. She's always running her hands along my sides and telling me how wonderful it is to have a slim trim husband again.

"Not only that, she even takes the initiative in our love-making sometimes, too. What a difference the loss of 55 pounds can make!"

So if you're fat and you have a sexual problem with your partner, when you get slim and trim on the non-glue-food diet, just as Gary R. did, ———

You'll gain these benefits

1. When you get down to your ideal weight, you'll be full of vim, vigor, vitality, and sexual go-power.
2. The non-glue-food diet improves glandular activity, and that's important for your glands are an essential part of your reproductive system.
3. The non-glue-food diet with its high protein content will enable you to perform all your body functions more effectively, but even more especially, the function of sex.
4. You can save your marriage and prevent a divorce when your sex relations with your partner return to normal.
5. You'll be able to fulfill one of your six basic needs when you are sexually satisfied.

6. You'll no longer feel restless, dissatisfied, and irritable in general, for satisfactory sexual love brings with it serenity, a feeling of contentment, and peace of mind. Sexual fulfillment may not bring you total happiness, but you can't have total happiness without sexual fulfillment either.

Sex begins in the dining room — not in the bedroom

Sexual prowess, stamina, and ability depend upon what you eat. The non-glue-food diet will give you that sexual stamina you need to have a normal and satisfactory sex relationship with your partner.

It is high in protein, fat, and Vitamin E, all three of which are needed for normal sexual activity. I have found that male impotence and female frigidity both respond extremely well to my non-glue-food diet.

This is not to imply that the non-glue-food diet will resolve the psychological problems that influence and affect your sex life. For instance, I know it is impossible to live on the mountain top emotionally every day. There will be those days when you're down in the valley of despair.

If you're depressed, if you're faced with serious financial troubles or business problems, if you're worried about your children for some reason, or if any other problem has you tied up in knots emotionally, it will influence your sexual activity tremendously.

But if you feel good physically, if you are in excellent health, your other problems won't seem as big to you. They won't seem completely impossible to solve.

Besides, I also know that sexual intercourse and making love can help you when you're down in the "dumps." When a man has been cruelly hurt, the arms of a loving wife can serve as his emotional security blanket. Or when a wife has been insulted or cut by some of her friends, a husband's love making lets her know that she's still very much wanted and needed.

Julie's experience

"Doctor, your non-glue-food diet saved my marriage," Julie told me. "After I had our second child, I started putting on weight and I couldn't seem to stop eating.

"Then Ken stopped paying attention to me completely. He stayed down at the office late every night and I'm sure he had a girl friend. He never made love to me for months at a time and when he did, he hurried to get it over with so he could get back in his own bed. The less attention he paid to me, the more I ate and the fatter I got. It was a vicious cycle.

"When Ken asked me for a divorce, I was panic stricken. But Karen L. said I should come to see you first before going to see my lawyer.

"How glad I am that I did. I've lost nearly 90 pounds on your non-glue-food diet and Ken never talks about divorce any more. In fact, I can't make him stay in his own bed. You'd think we were still on our honeymoon the way he acts!"

Protein is necessary for sexual activity

If you will remember, protein is necessary to replace and repair body tissue and to form new cells, including male sperm cells and the female ova. Remember also that man-made carbohydrates, the glue-foods, are never used by your body to build muscle tissue, blood, or bone, or to form new cells of any kind, including those male sperm cells and the female eggs the ova.

Therefore, any diet that is low in protein and high in man-made carbohydrates will result in a lowered and inadequate sexual activity. With that kind of diet, there is no fuel to stoke the fire of sexual desire. In fact, without an adequate protein intake, there can be no sexual desire and very little sexual activity.

But a diet that is high in protein works exactly the opposite way. It stimulates and increases sexual desire and sexual activity. The best sources of protein, if you will recall, are meat, poultry, fish and seafood, eggs, and cheese. Excellent sources of vegetable proteins are leafy vegetables.

"Since Beatrice and I have been on your non-glue-food diet, we've found our sexual desires have increased greatly," Omer told me. "Before when we were eating a lot of glue-foods, once a week was it. Now it's every other night, thanks to your non-glue-food diet, Doc."

Proteins are made up of amino acids

Proteins cannot be absorbed from your digestive tract into your blood steam and on to that part of the body where they are needed until they are broken down into *amino acids*. Once these amino acids are absorbed into your body, they are then reassembled into the proteins that make up the muscle tissue, blood, bone, and other cells of your body. These amino acids are also used to manufacture your sex hormones. Two of them are absolutely essential to your sexual activity and sexual well-being.

Tryptophane. Unless a woman has enough tryptophane in her diet she can never bear a child. The lack of tryptophane is also a calamity for a man. His testicles will degenerate because of this amino acid deficiency. The best sources of tryptophane on the non-glue-food diet are cheese, eggs, liver, kidney, and leafy green vegetables.

Arginine. This amino acid is often called the *fatherhood amino acid.* If there is a deficiency of this amino acid in the diet, a complete loss or a marked decrease in the sex drive of either a man or a woman is the end result. A lack of arginine causes impotence, frigidity, and sterility. It also causes a decrease in the formation of male sperm cells which are 80 percent arginine. The best sources of arginine on the non-glue-food diet are eggs, liver, seafood — especially sardines — and cheese.

Seeds and sexual desire

Down through the ages people have thought certain foods had magical qualities to improve their sexual abilities. These foods were called *aphrodisiacs.*

If any foods deserve this title they would be sesame seeds and sunflower seeds. Since both of them contain the two amino acids — tryptophane and arginine — that are so essential to sexual desire and sexual activity, they are much more deserving to be called aphrodisiacs than are oysters or bull testicles, camel's hump or goat's eyes, or any other strange or exotic spice or seasoning.

Sesame seeds and sunflower seeds also contain lecithin, a major deficiency of which can lead to sexual impotence and frigidity. Not only that, these two seeds are really a complete all-around food.

They are a rich source of the B Vitamins, minerals, and unsaturated fats. While raising your sexual drive, they are also nourishing your entire body. You can safely add them to your list of non-glue-foods to snack on for they're much more beneficial to you than are the man-made carbohydrates, the glue-foods.

"I don't think eating sesame seeds and sunflower seeds has increased the amount of my sexual activity," Tom told me, "but I do know this. Since I've been eating them instead of glue-foods, I get a lot deeper and fuller satisfaction from sexual intercourse."

Vitamin E is also necessary for normal sexual function

Although it is called the *sex vitamin,* scientists do not yet know exactly how Vitamin E works to affect reproduction and sexual desire. They do know, however, that it is one of the vitamins man must have if he is going to stay healthy sexually.

They also know that it is necessary for the normal functioning and health of the reproductive glands and organs and to the maintenance of sexual potency, for it has been shown by laboratory experiments that Vitamin E deficiency in animals results in testicular degeneration and sterility.

The best sources of Vitamin E on the non-glue-food diet are the unsaturated vegetable oils you use on your green salads, leafy green vegetables, meat, eggs, and the Vitamin E supplement I ask you to add to your diet.

An excellent source of Vitamin E would be wheat germ, but you will not be able to get it in bread or cereals because of our modern milling and baking processes that remove the wheat germ and the Vitamin E to keep the product from becoming rancid and spoiled.

Don't be fooled by the statements on the label or the wrapper that say *enriched* or *fortified* either. A few *synthetic* B Vitamins — Niacin, Thiamine, and Riboflavin — and some iron are put in the bread during the manufacturing process, but the Vitamin E that was been taken out is never returned. Nor is it ever put back in cereals by the cereal manufacturers either.

Taking away all the natural vitamins and minerals and putting back only a few synthetics is comparable to being robbed of your car and your wallet and then being given a bus token by the robber to get home on because he feels sorry for you.

Besides, as you already know, cereals and bread are glue-foods because of the flour, sugar, and starch they contain so they are just not for you. Not only that, even if you could eat packaged cereals and bakery bread on the non-glue-food diet, I wouldn't want you to do so. You could eat them all day long and not get enough wheat germ or Vitamin E to whet your sex appetite at all or do you one bit of good in any other way either.

Results of the non-glue-food diet speak for themselves

A great many of my patients tell me that the non-glue-food diet has not only improved the quantity, but also the quality, of their sex relations. Just for instance, J. R. tells me this: "Used to be, Doc, that when I climbed into bed at the end of a hard day, all I wanted to do was sleep. I was just too tired to even think of making love with my wife. Not any more. Instead of once every couple of weeks or so, we find ourselves reliving our honeymoon days.

"Not only that, Doc, I find I can now sustain an erection for a much longer time and thus prolong intercourse which helps my wife to fully reach her climax. Your non-glue-food diet has really been a life-saver for us, Doc. It kept our marriage from going completely on the rocks."

Another one of my patients, who recently became a grandmother for the fourth time, told me that for nearly six years she had considered her active sex life to be over and done with. Her general health was good and she was not more than 10 pounds overweight. However, she told me that her sexual desires had dwindled away and she was so unresponsive that her husband had finally stopped making any overtures to her at all.

"I wasn't overly concerned about our lack of sexual intercourse until I noticed that my husband had become extremely attentive to younger women at some of the social functions we attended," she told me. "Then I realized that I had to do something about the situation or run the risk of losing my husband. So I came to you. After just a few weeks on your non-glue-food diet along with the Vitamin E supplement, I began to notice a definite change in my sexual desires toward my husband. I wanted him to make love to me again. It's only been two months now, but Adam and I are once again enjoying normal sexual relations. I believe our marriage is now back on solid ground."

If you find that your sex desires have slackened, if you're spending more time in charity or women's club work, if you're staying at the office working late each night, or if you're spending more evenings entertaining clients when you could be home making love with your wife — get on the non-glue-food diet quick before it's too late.

Six high protein meals a day will increase your sexual drive and stamina

Six high protein meals a day will do much more than just

help you get rid of your excess fat. They will also increase your sexual efficiency. Scientists have discovered that people tire less easily and they they can work harder and longer on six small meals a day than they can on three large ones. Sexual intercourse is also physical exercise. In fact, you use about the same amount of energy when you make love as you do when you take a half-hour walk.

If you plan on sexual activity to top off the day, then your most important meal of the day will be your last one. Don't make the mistake of overeating if you want to make love later on that night. If you've eaten too much or if you've eaten too late, you'll go to bed with a bloated too-tight too-full feeling in your belly, and sex will be the last thing in the world you'll be interested in.

Learn to take the proper approach to sex. After all, it is one of the most important parts of your life and it should not be treated lightly or regarded as a casual matter. Proper preparation and anticipation of what's to come is half the fun. And eating the proper food is part of that important preparation.

Take a professional athlete, for example. He will usually eat a good high protein meal of steak and eggs before a game. He will then rest for a couple of hours so he can be at his proper physical and mental peak when it really counts.

You would do well to follow his example, even down to the steak and eggs, in preparing yourself for making love. If you can't take in six small meals a day, then make sure your snacks between meals are high protein foods such as beef, chicken, eggs, cheese, etc. You can also nibble on some sunflower seeds.

A married couple in their early sixties came to me for help, having heard of my non-glue-food diet's success from some friends of theirs. Neither of the two were excessively fat. That was not their problem at all. They had come to me for help with their sex life.

After their children had grown and gone, Bill and Mary found that having the privacy of their early married life again was not exactly the exciting adventure they had hoped it would be.

When they came to see me, their sexual intercourse had dwindled down to once every couple of weeks or so.

They were fond of each other, but they no longer felt a strong physical desire for each other. They felt that something might be wrong with them physically and they were wise enough to want to prevent any conflict or deep misunderstanding arising from their sexual inactivity.

Both of them were in general good health, although they lacked energy and vitality. They were always tired and worn-out, they said, but they had blamed that on their advancing years. I told them it had to be more than that since they were only in their early sixties.

I placed them on my non-glue-food diet along with the vitamin and mineral supplements I recommend for all my fat patients, including Vitamin E. Since Bill was retired and had no regular office hours to keep, I also asked them to schedule their meals so they could eat at least 6 times a day.

In less than 60 days they told me they felt like honeymooners again. They were both much more alert and had a greater amount of energy. Life had taken on a deeper meaning for them and it seemed to be well worth living again to both of them.

How the non-glue-food diet physically affects your sex organs

Not only does the non-glue-food diet stimulate your desires and your capacity for sexual activity and furnish you with more energy at the same time, it also causes definite physical changes to take place in the actual functioning of your sex organs during intercourse.

Male patients, for instance, tell me that they are able to achieve a much stiffer and harder erection than previously. They also say they can sustain an erection for a much longer period of time than before. This is, of course, highly beneficial to both partners.

Female patients find that they are much more sensitive and responsive during foreplay and during actual intercourse. They also note a marked increase in vaginal secretions. This is also highly beneficial to both partners.

Both men and women patients report to me that they experience a heightened awareness of their own bodies and the bodies of their partners. In almost every single case, they experience a much more satisfying orgasm than ever before.

Other vitamins that influence your sexual activity

Although Vitamin E is known as the sex vitamin, some of the other vitamins also play an important part in sexual function, desire, and activity. I'd like to discuss those vitamins quite briefly. I will cover primarily their relationships to sexual activity. Their other functions will be discussed in the next chapter.

Vitamin A. The reproductive organs are all protected with epithelial tissues that depend upon Vitamin A for their good health. When there is plenty of Vitamin A in your diet, these epithelial cells can do their job properly. They secrete a mucous fluid that bathes and disinfects the mucous membranes of the reproductive organs, killing foreign bacteria. But when Vitamin A is missing from your diet, or when it is deficient, these cells dry up and infection is the end result.

Vitamin A is also needed for normal reproduction. Scientific study with animals has proven that conclusively. For instance, in one experiment Vitamin A was withheld from the diet of mother pigs before conception and during the pregnancy. Every single pig in the litter was born blind. Many had no eyeballs at all. Some had club feet, a harelip, and a cleft palate.

Then Vitamin A was added to their diet and the very same mother pigs were used in the next experiment. They were all made pregnant again, but this time their litters all contained normal healthy offspring, just from the addition of Vitamin A to their diet.

It has also been found that Vitamin A is necessary in human beings for normal sexual activity. It is essential for the proper functioning of the sex glands, especially the testes. It insures vitality in cell growth, resistance to infection, delays senility, and increases longevity. Vitamin A will help prolong your active sex life.

If you lack Vitamin A in your diet, you run the risk of inflammation of your reproductive organs and lack of normal sex gland activity. Your children could be born with a harelip, a cleft palate, or a club foot.

Good food sources of Vitamin A on the non-glue-food diet are leafy green vegetables, liver, eggs, cheese, and butter.

Vitamin B complex. The Vitamin B complex consists of several B Vitamins. I will discuss them all under one heading to conserve both time and space. I'm sure you're familiar with the names of at least three of them: thiamine, riboflavin, and niacin.

The wisdom of using a natural instead of a synthetic vitamin is most evident with the B Complex. People who buy synthetics get only a few of the B Vitamins, usually thiamine, riboflavin, and niacin — the same three that bakeries always put back in their bread.

They are always disappointed with the results they get, for the point is there can be no such thing as a deficiency in only one of the B Vitamins. If you are deficient in one of them, you will be deficient in all of them. When you correct only one vitamin deficiency, the lack of the other vitamins will become even more apparent.

If Vitamin B1 (Thiamine) is in short supply in your diet, there will be a reduction in the amount of sex hormones your body manufactures. A lowered sexual desire and capacity results.

If Vitamin B2 (Riboflavin) is deficient in your diet, you will feel a diminution of energy and vitality, including a lessened sexual desire and potential.

Niacin and Vitamin B12 are especially important to the proper functioning of the entire nervous system upon which the enjoyment of sexual relations depends.

There are still other B Vitamins in the complex, but they do not seem to be as influential on your sexual activity as these are. Good good sources on the non-glue-food diet for the entire

B Complex are all the meats including liver, poultry, seafood, eggs, cheese, and all green vegetables.

The entire Vitamin B Complex is water soluble, just as is Vitamin C. If you cook your green vegetables and throw away the cooking water, chances are you've lost all the Vitamin B and Vitamin C they originally contained. That's why green salads are often better than green vegetables that are cooked. It's also another potent reason to take a natural multi-vitamin multi-mineral supplement along with your non-glue-food diet.

Although there is no doubt in my mind that all the other vitamins are important to normal sexual function and activity, their major functions seem more related to other body activities, so I will discuss some of them in the next chapter.

Before leaving this section on vitamins, though, I would like to point out that environmental pollution, drugs, pesticides, and food additives that prevent spoilage can destroy the natural vitamins in the foods you eat.

Dr. T. Keith Murray, Chief of the Nutritional Research Division of the Canadian Food and Drug Directorate in Ottawa, Canada, says there is a tremendous incidence of Vitamin A deficiency among Canadians. He also says, "I can see no reason why the same condition would not be likely to occur in the United States as well."

Dr. Murray suspects that environmental pollution, drugs, pesticides, and food additives that prevent spoilage are to blame. He thinks these factors have cut down on our ability to use efficiently the Vitamin A that we take in, or in some cases, that we might even be burning up too fast in our bodies.

If environmental pollution, pesticides, and food additives can destroy Vitamin A, it is logical to assume they could destroy all the rest of the vitamins, too, for Vitamin A is much more stable and less likely to be destroyed than the Vitamin B Complex or Vitamin C.

That is why it is really no longer possible for a doctor to say that certain foods are good sources of certain vitamins unless he actually knows specifically the condition of the soil in which those foods were grown.

That's still another reason why I ask all my patients to play it safe and take a *natural* multi-vitamin multi-mineral supplement. I simply know of no other way to be absolutely sure.

Why minerals are important for sexual power

Most people are vitamin conscious, but very few are mineral conscious. Yet without the body-building, body-regulating minerals, vitamins could not be used by your body. They would be completely worthless to you.

Scientific studies of the average diet indicate that our average daily foods are extremely short of minerals. Minerals in the right proportion will give you firm bones, sound teeth, steady nerves, strong muscles, a reliable and regular heartbeat, good posture, a keen mind, healthy vital organs, and an extension of your prime of life.

The functions of the various minerals would completely fill a book three or four times as big as this one. For this reason, I will only touch briefly upon the most important ones.

Every single one of these minerals is needed for normal sexual activity, either directly or indirectly. Take calcium and phosphorus, just for example. The simple fact that they help to ward off fatigue means they would be useful to you in raising your sexual stamina, prowess, and ability.

Calcium helps to build strong teeth and bones. It aids in the clotting of blood. It also prevents fatigue. It cannot be absorbed from your digestive tract into your bloodstream unless Vitamin D is present.

Signs of calcium deficiency, other than poor bone and tooth formation, are nervousness, muscle cramps, and rapid heartbeat.

Certain drugs or foods can prevent the proper absorption of calcium from the digestive tract. Experiments show that chocolate and cocoa will prevent calcium assimilation. White bread is also highly suspect.

Sources of calcium on the non-glue-food diet are leafy green vegetables, cheese, eggs, and seafood. If you do not have to be concerned about your excess fat, milk is also an excellent source of calcium.

Phosphorus works like calcium and in conjunction with it. It is just as vital to body health as calcium is. In fact, the absorption process is the same for both minerals.

In the bones and teeth, phosphorus acts as a hardening agent to give them strength. It also prevents fatigue. In the soft tissues, phosphorus is found in the structure of every cell nucleus. It is also found in all sex cells and nerve cells. Brain tissues are also rich in phosphorus.

Sources of phosphorus on the non-glue-food diet are all the protein foods: meat, poultry, fish, seafood, eggs, and cheese.

Iron is said to be the chief of all minerals for every single cell in your body depends on it for oxygen — the breath of life. A shortage of iron causes anemia and means constant fatigue and a loss of vitality and ambition. If you are deficient in iron, you simply are worn-out and exhausted all the time. You don't even have the energy to do your daily work, let alone indulge in the pleasures of sexual intercourse.

Sources of iron on the non-glue-food diet include leafy green vegetables, eggs, and meat — especially liver.

Iodine is essential for the proper functioning of the thyroid gland, the chief regulator of your body's metabolic rate. If you are deficient in iodine, your reflexes will be sluggish and slow. It will be hard for you to think clearly and concentrate on your work. You will have little interest in anything in life, especially sexual intercourse and love-making.

On the non-glue-food diet, a good source of iodine would be fish and seafood. Today most salt is also iodized to prevent an iodine deficiency.

Another excellent source of iodine and other trace minerals needed by your body is seaweed or sea kelp. A good commercial product is *Parkelp,* made by the Philip R. Park Company of San Pedro, California. You can buy Parkelp at your local health food store.

Copper must be present before your body can use iron. It is necessary, therefore, to prevent anemia. If you are deficient in copper, not only will you get anemia, but you will also have a general weakness and an impaired respiration. You will have no desire at all for sex. The best sources on the non-glue-food diet for copper are liver, fish, seafood, eggs, and leafy green vegetables.

Sodium is one mineral that helps maintain the proper acid-base balance in your body. It also helps to keep calcium in solution so it can be transported by your blood stream to the tissues that need it. Sodium helps your body cells select the foods they need and pull them out of the blood stream. It also helps your body cells and tissues to get rid of their waste products. The best source of sodium is, of course, common table salt (sodium chloride).

Chlorine is used by the body in its digestive juice as hydrochloric acid. It acts as a cleansing agent for the body by destroying invading bacteria in your digestive tract. Chlorine is also important to help regulate all nervous activity in your body to include sexual activity. This is especially important to you if you are a man, for erection of the penis is controlled through the involuntary nervous system. It's also important to you if you're the man's wife.

Potassium is another balancing mineral. It works in conjunction with sodium in attracting nourishment from the blood stream for your body cells. It also helps your body cells get rid of their waste products. It assists in keeping all your muscles in proper tone and it is important for the proper functioning of your liver and kidneys.

Even a slight deficiency of potassium leads to slow growth, constipation, and a strange nervous ailment that develops into irritability and insomnia. If your body's potassium is low, your heart beat will become slow and irregular. Your kidneys can become enlarged and damaged. I would think it needless to say that when your health is that bad, you could have no interest at all in sexual activity.

The best sources of potassium on the non-glue-food diet are leafy green vegetables, tomatoes, cucumbers, and fruit.

Magnesium is necessary for proper formation and functioning of your nervous system, your brain, and your lungs. Children who lack the proper amount of magnesium will be mentally retarded. A good source of magnesium is found in leafy green vegetables where it is a component part of that magical substance, *chlorophyll.*

Sulphur is a blood and liver conditioner and cleanser. It promotes the secretion of bile and is an aid in absorbing other minerals from the digestive tract. It is found in protein foods, cabbage, and Brussels sprouts.

Manganese is absolutely necessary for normal sexual activity. A deficiency of manganese can cause a complete loss of interest in sexual intercourse, more so than the absence of any other mineral perhaps. Its absence in the diet interferes with the maternal instinct and normal reproductive functions.

The best sources of manganese on the non-glue-food diet are leafy green vegetables.

Trace Minerals are other essential elements found in minute quantities in plant and animal life. *Silicon* is one such trace mineral. *Zinc* is another. I would not begin to attempt to cover them all or discuss their various functions here. There are simply far too many for me to attempt to do that.

To wrap up this section on minerals, I would like to say that if you take 3 tablets daily of *V-Complette,* the natural multi-vitamin multi-mineral product made by Schiff as well as some *Parkelp* tablets, you'll be absolutely certain of getting all the minerals you need to carry on all your normal body activities, including especially the function of sex.

Why age need not be a barrier to sex

It is not true that sex can be enjoyed only while you're young. That is a myth. You can enjoy sex at almost any age in life if you are healthy and free from disease.

If you are to enjoy your older years to the fullest, you should follow the non-glue-food diet, walk to keep your muscles toned up and to help your circulation, maintain a positive and active mental attitude toward life, and *engage regularly in sexual activity.*

A man's virility does not normally decline to any great extent as long as he is physically fit and in good health until after he is 75. If you give up sex before then, you're losing a lot of the pleasure in life that is rightfully yours if you're a man.

Not only that, you're depriving your wife from enjoying the pleasures of sex at the same time. There is no indication that a woman ever loses her ability to enjoy sexual activity, no matter what her age, as long as she is physiologically capable of engaging in intercourse.

Of course, there will be times when an erection might not come to you as quickly as it did when you were younger. But that doesn't mean you're all washed up. It could mean that your system is simply overloaded with all the toxic poisons of the glue-foods.

A few months on the non-glue-food diet with its high protein content supplemented by Vitamin E and minerals can make you strong and active again sexually. Your sex drive does not have to disappear just because your hair is turning gray.

Plan your sexual activities

Young or old, you would do well to plan your sexual activities in advance. If tonight is the night, then you ought to prepare for it as carefully as you would get ready for a dance, or a party, or a night out on the town. Far too many couples treat their sexual relationships in a casual off-hand manner, and then wonder why they have problems develop later on in life.

If you're a woman, don't take your sexual partner for granted. Make yourself attractive for him. Bathe, perfume, and powder before going to your bed. And for God's sake — skip the rollers, the curlers, the pins, the face-creams, and the nightcap. That's the fastest way to turn off a man's sexual desires that I know of. It's also a quick shortcut to Reno or Las Vegas.

If you're a man, shower and shave and splash on the good smelly lotions. Sprinkle on the powder, too. Your wife will love it. If you've shaved once already that morning, shave again. Twice a day for the sake of sex isn't going to kill you. No woman wants a scratchy face rubbing her cheek or nuzzling her breast.

I tell all my patients with sexual problems to prepare for their evening pleasures as if it were the last time they could ever have sexual intercourse with their partner, and therefore, they should do their utmost to make it the best one ever for both of them. They all tell me it has helped their attitude toward sex and their sexual partner tremendously.

Keep variety in your love making

I don't expect you to indulge in bedroom acrobatics if you're in your sixties or so, but there's no harm in trying a variety of positions as long as both of you are willing to experiment. What you do in the privacy of your bedroom is nobody's business but yours. It is not the business of your children, your minister, or anyone else, for that matter.

However, don't use any position that is in the least uncomfortable or that places your body in any sort of physical strain. If you are the least bit uncomfortable in the sex act you will become completely ineffective.

One older couple in their late sixties, both of whom are patients of mine, enjoy sexual activity much more than some married people I've seen who are in their thirties and forties.

T. L. tells me they prepare themselves for intercourse as if it were a festive occasion to be celebrated. They spend plenty of time in the bathroom together bathing, showering, shaving, powdering, perfuming, and so on. T. L. says they have a large Japenese style bath that both of them can use at the same time. They soap and rinse each other to stimulate their sexual desires.

Then when they go to bed they massage each other completely with a light and fragrant disappearing body oil. "By the time we finish that, nothing could keep us apart," T. L. says. "If our children ever found out how we prepare for sexual intercourse, I suppose they would think we were just a couple of senile old perverts, but as far as I'm concerned, it's none of their business.

"We enjoy each other and we bring each other more pleasure

than we were able to do when we were back in our twenties and thirties. We've kept our marriage intact for nearly 50 years now by loving each other this way. And that's a lot more than a couple of my own kids can say."

I really think T. L. summed it all up right there in his last paragraph much better that I could ever do, so I'm not even going to try. Instead, I'm going to move right on the the next chapter where you'll learn ——

HOW THE NON-GLUE-FOOD DIET CAN MAKE YOU LOOK AND FEEL 10 TO 20 YEARS YOUNGER

6. How the non-glue-food diet can make you look and feel 10 to 20 years younger

Have you ever seen people every so often who look much, much younger to you than they actually are? I'm sure you have; I have, too. What was it about them that you noticed that actually made them seem much younger than their true calendar years? Was it their skin, their complexion, posture, teeth, eyes, spring in their step, the sports or physical activities they participated in, their mental attitude? Or was it all of these things plus a certain mysterious indefinable something about that person that made him seem much younger to you?

Here's the key to how old you look and feel

I'm sure when you've seen people like that, you've wondered why they were so fortunate to be able to keep their youthful appearance, especially when most people look their age and more.

First off, let me tell you why most people look their age, and oftentimes, more than their age. Then you'll be much better able to understand why a rare few look so much younger than they actually are. Most people, whether they're extremely heavy or not, show their age and more because of an excessive consumption of glue-foods, especially sugar. Sugar is the real "killer" of youthfulness.

In 1750 the average person ate only four pounds of sugar a year. Only the rich could afford more than that. In 1840, nearly a hundred years later, the average consumption of sugar was still low — 20 pounds a year. But today the average American consumes 175 pounds of sugar each year.

Why is this so important? *Because excessive sugar consumption upsets the metabolic processes in the body*. That is a proven scientific fact. Excessive sugar intake continually stimulates the pancreas to produce insulin until finally it becomes trigger-happy. Then you have a disturbed carbohydrate metabolism in the body.

When your carbohydrate metabolism is abnormal, you will age prematurely; you will get old long before your time

Premature aging — and the fatigue and physical exhaustion that go with it — is a sign of an abnormal carbohydrate metabolism just as is excessive fat. And, *an abnormal carbohydrate metabolism results from excessive sugar consumption*. Therefore, by logical deduction and scientific reasoning we can say that *excessive sugar consumption causes premature aging* whether you're thin or fat. Let me show you that a little more clearly with a formula like this:

1. Excessive sugar consumption (A) causes an abnormal carbohydrate metabolism (B). (Fact)
2. An abnormal carbohydrate metabolism (B) causes

premature aging (C). (Fact)
3. Therefore, excessive sugar consumption (A) causes premature aging (C). (Deduction or conclusion)

If A causes B and B causes C, then A also causes C.

Now then, if excessive consumption of sugar causes premature aging, you should now know why a person can look 10 to 20 years younger than he actually is. The answer is so simple. That person consumes no man-made carbohydrates. He stays completely away from glue-foods. That's why he looks so young. If you don't believe that, ask him. You'll find out soon enough that it's true.

The non-glue-food diet can make you look and feel much younger

A good many of my patients look much younger than they actually are now that they're eating properly and have regained their health on my non-glue-food diet. I met one of them at lunch recently. She's an excellent example, so let me tell you about her.

The case of Katherine — at 50 years of age

Katherine has been a patient of mine for over 3 years, although now she comes in only once a month for a check-up. When she first came to see me, she was one of the most despondent persons I'd ever seen enter my office.

She had just turned fifty, her children were all gone from home, her husband had retired and was spending more and more time on the golf course and at the Executive Athletic Club — which welcomes both sexes, incidentally, — and Katherine felt more and more alone and badly neglected. She felt she was no longer wanted or needed by anyone.

So she had turned to food for solace just as an alcoholic will turn to liquor to blot out the reality of the present moment. And the pounds started to pile on. The fatter she became, the more and more time her husband spent away from home, and the more neglected she felt. She was caught up in a vicious cycle from which she could not seem to escape.

Then one day a sympathetic friend, who'd gone through the same trying circumstances before she lost 60 pounds in 8 months on my non-glue-food diet, told Katherine about me. So Katherine came to see me the next day as a last resort, for she felt that no one could possibly help her or do anything for her.

I insisted that she follow the same exact procedure I told you about way back in Chapter 1. I knew that with her negative attitude my non-glue-food diet would not work unless she could really understand *why* she wanted to reduce so she could motivate herself to do so. I knew that without the proper motivation, she would not stick to the non-glue-food diet for even a week.

Katherine stayed away from my office for nearly 3 weeks, but when she did come back I knew at once she meant business. Her eyes were different. They had a steely hard determined look in them. And the tone of her voice was strong and firm. I could tell that her mental attitude had undergone a tremendous change.

"I've been withdrawing from life, Doctor," she said. "I've been miserable and lonely and afraid. I've been scared to death of losing my husband. I've felt unwanted and neglected. I even thought my own children didn't love me any more.

"I realize that's not true, but I also know that I must make a new life for myself that's not dependent on any of them. They have their own lives to live and so have I. I want to start living again. Trouble is, I don't even know how or where to start. Please show me how, Doctor. I need help. . .will you help me?"

I knew that with Katherine's positive mental *attitude* and her changed outlook on life she would be an excellent patient and she certainly has been. She dropped from 197 pounds down to 126, a total loss of 71 pounds in less than a year. And as those pounds melted away, she became more beautiful and looked younger every single day.

Katherine is now 54 and has become a grandmother twice since she became a patient of mine several years ago. When I met her at our Club at lunch recently, had I not known, I would have guessed her to be 35.

Today her skin and her complexion resemble that of a healthy 20-year old girl. Her posture is perfect and she has the measurements of a model with 38-24-36. Her belly is flat and firm and strong and you'd never guess that she's borne five children or that she's ever been fat.

There is a lively healthy spring to her step. She's taken up golf, bowling, and even tennis, although I've told her not to get carried away there. I don't like to see any person over 50 — fat or thin — get too ambitious on the tennis court no matter how good their general health is, for tennis and snow shoveling fit into about the same category because of the sudden heavy demands on the heart.

Katherine's face seems to light up and her eyes glow and sparkle with both the joy of the present moment and anticipation of the future. That you don't often see in a person over 50. But her mental attitude toward life just couldn't be any better.

And her husband, Jim? Did you ask if he's spending time on the golf course by himself or at the Executive Athletic Club all alone? If you had a wife who looked like Katherine, would you leave her alone? I wouldn't and neither does Jim. When I saw Katherine yesterday, he was sitting right there beside her, looking very proud, very jealous, and possessive.

You, too, as a woman can look and feel 10 to 20 years younger yourself, no matter how old you are. In fact, when you get rid of your exeess fat, — — —

You'll gain these benefits

1. Men will want to whistle at you.
2. You'll be mistaken for your daughter.
3. You won't have to make excuses to anyone for your figure.
4. You can jump in the pool and swim without effort.
5. You don't have to wear stripes to look thin.

6. You can wear bright-colored clothes.
7. You'll have more energy, vitality, pep, and go-power.
8. Your complexion will be clear — your hair will shine.
9. There'll be spring in your heart and a spring in your step.
10. You'll be free of a myriad of aches and pains.
11. You'll sleep much better without tranquilizers.
12. You'll be regular without drugs or laxatives.
13. You'll add years to your life and life to your years.

Techniques you can use to gain these benefits

Although the non-glue-food diet will make you feel better, look better, and restore you to vibrant health and vigorous vitality, there are some additional active and positive measures you can use yourself that will help you look 10 to 20 years younger. I'd like to spend the rest of this chapter discussing a few of these methods with you.

How to have a youthful skin and a radiant complexion

Your skin can make you look much older than you really are, especially if you've been eating glue-foods for a long time. But after only a short while on the non-glue-food diet it will recover its youthful appearance.

Skin is protein and if it is to be alive and glowing with radiant health, you must have plenty of protein in your diet to feed it. As you already know, the non-glue-food diet is loaded with protein. Not only that, I've encouraged you throughout this entire book to eat all the protein you could possibly want.

"You look absolutely radiant, Maxine," I said to one of my patients yesterday. "Your skin is absolutely flawless now; it looks so healthy."

"Thanks to you, Doctor," she said. "Remember what it looked like before I started on your non-glue-food diet? You couldn't have said that a few months ago when I was eating sugar and starch instead of protein. When I look in the mirror now, I feel 10 years younger than I am. It's amazing to me how many good things have happened since I stopped eating glue-foods."

Unsaturated fatty acids in your diet are also necessary if you are to have a glowing beautiful and youthful skin. And as you also know well, the non-glue-food diet contains them, too, in the form of corn oil, margarine, safflower oil, and so on.

Psoriasis, acne, and *eczema* all improve when unsaturated fats are added to the diet. Linoleic acid, the major constituent of safflower oil, is especially helpful for the problems of eczema and acne. This is another reason I recommend the addition of safflower oil capsules to your non-glue-food diet.

Vitamins and minerals are also important for a healthy skin

Dermatologists as well as nutritionists have found that certain vitamins and minerals are fundamentally important to skin health. Let me cover those right now and if you've had any lingering doubts about taking a multi-vitamin multi-mineral supplement each day, I think they'll be completely and finally dispelled. Following is a listing of the important Vitamins you should have in your diet or supplementation:

Vitamin A

Vitamin A is necessary for a healthy and youthful skin. If it is missing from your diet or if it is deficient, you will be prone to have numerous skin infections. Pimples, blackheads, and boils will be quite common. Vitamin A also delays senility and increases longevity, a point I consider well worth noting.

Vitamin B2

Vitamin B$_2$ (Riboflavin) is often referred to as the *youth vitamin.* It is absolutely necessary if you have to have a healthy skin. This was proven in one study conducted by Doctors Sebrell and Butler of the United States Public Health Service.

These two doctors experimented with 18 young women who volunteered to go on a diet that was deficient in Vitamin B$_2$. In only four months the oil glands in their face could no longer function properly.

An excessively oily condition appeared on the forehead, nose, and chin. Their lips became sore and red and later on cracked and peeled. They developed big cracks in the corners of the mouth. Oily scabs sprang up at the corners of the nose and on the upper lips.

Niacin — the pellagra preventing vitamin that I will discuss in just a moment — was given to them, but no improvement was noted. In fact, the condition grew steadily worse. Then they were given Vitamin B_2 (Riboflavin) and the condition was corrected almost overnight as if by magic.

Niacin

Niacin is still another vitamin of the B Complex. A deficiency of Niacin in the diet, if marked, can result in pellagra, a disease still quite common in the South. It is marked by diarrhea, dermatitis, and dementia or insanity.

In experiments of the United States Public Health Service, volunteer prisoners were fed the common diet that was popular in the South to see if they would develop pellagra. They were to be completely pardoned if they completed the experiment.

They were allowed to have all the corn bread, sweet potatoes, corn syrup, dried peas, dried beans, and cured or salted down-fat pork (sow belly) that they wanted. In only a few short weeks pellagra appeared. It was quickly cured with fresh meat — including liver — and fresh vegetables.

I think you can see immediately that the pellagra-producing diet was basically a glue-food diet. Now you may not have a serious enough Niacin deficiency to develop pellagra, but it can still be a contributing factor to any dermatitis that you might possibly have.

Vitamin B_6

Vitamin B_6 (Pyridoxine) is also necessary for a healthy complexion. If you have a deficiency of it, you can develop an excessively oily skin. Contrary to what so many people believe, an oily skin is not due to too much oil in the diet, but it is due primarily to some kind of vitamin, mineral, fat, or protein deficiency.

Pantothenic Acid

Pantothenic Acid is still another of the Vitamin B Complex. Its absence or deficiency can also cause skin infections and premature aging of your body.

Skin tone and condition also depend upon many minerals being present in your diet. However, because of my time and space limitations, I'll only mention one mineral, *sulphur,* for it is often referred to as the *beauty mineral.*

Sulphur is a must in your diet for without it your skin will be dry and lifeless; your hair will be dull and lusterless; your fingernails will crack and deteriorate.

The wrong kind of soap can also cause skin irritations

Some soaps contain chemicals and detergents that can cause serious irritation to your skin. For many years, I was troubled with a slight scalp infection that seemed to come and go dependent, I thought, upon my moods and emotions. So I marked it down as a minor psychosomatic problem. I was to find out that was not so.

One day my wife happened to buy a new kind of soap from her Amway distributor. It was called a *Glycerine and Honey Complexion Bar.* I liked the smell of it and I liked what they said about it on the box. So out of curiosity I tried it as a shampoo. To my surprise, my scalp infection disappeared and I've never been troubled with it since.

When your body gets the proper nutrition, you won't get sick

I'd like to point out to you here that when your body tissues are in good health, when your cells are receiving the vital nourishment that they need, your chances of getting sick from any sort of bacterial invasion are practically nil.

My garbage can example

Let me explain that in more detail by what I call the *garbage can example.* Just suppose you had an empty but dirty garbage can on your back porch. It had no garbage in it, but it still had a few food particles. In other words, it had been emptied, but not washed. Naturally it would be surrounded with flies for *flies always go where the food is.*

Of course you don't like flies on your back porch so you get out your fly swatter and you kill them all. But an hour later you find your back porch is again filled with flies so you get out your fly swatter once more and again you kill them all. But an hour later you find the same situation exists, so you get out your fly swatter and you. . . .

Is this what you would do? Of course not. You'd take your garbage can and wash it inside and out with soap and water. You'd remove every last bit of food waste until it was sparkling clean. Then you'd spray it with a good disinfectant to destroy any food particles you might possibly have missed. Then when you set it out on your back porch again, you'd be no longer troubled with flies.

Because you'd killed all the flies with your fly swatter? No indeed. The flies are still very much alive, but they've gone somewhere else to eat. When there's no food to eat, they will not come around to bother you for *flies only go where the food is.*

Every animal or bird or fish or bug is exactly the same as the fly. Every living creature spends 95 percent of its waking moments in search of food — unless it is domesticated, of course, like a cat or a dog, and knows it doesn't have to hunt for food to stay alive.

Bacteria go where the food is, too

The bacteria that try to invade your body are the same. *They go where the food is, too.* If all your body cells and tissues are alive and glowing with vigor and vitality because you're feeding them the proper nutrients — proteins, fats, vitamins, and minerals — then the bacteria have no food to eat and they will die without causing you to get sick. Bacteria cannot eat your live healthy tissue cells for food. *Bacteria can eat only dead and dying body tissues.*

Your body even manufactures its own internal disinfectants to destroy bacteria. The stomach makes hydrochloric acid and all the other cells that form your various mucous membranes secrete a thin antiseptic fluid that contains a bacteria-killing disinfectant.

If somehow the bacteria do penetrate this first line of defense and get into your body, the battle will be taken up by the white blood cells in your blood stream.

But without the proper foods in your diet, your body will be unable to perform any of these functions. It simply won't be able to manufacture its own antiseptic fluids nor will your white blood cells be strong enough to defeat the invading organisms.

If you're eating glue-foods that cannot be used to build muscle tissue, blood, or bone cells — if you are allowing your body cells to die because of a lack of the proper nutrients in your diet — you can bet that you will get sick for you'll have all kinds of food material for the bacteria to feed on.

Just remember that bacteria are no different at all from any other living creature. They are just smaller, that's all. They, too, must eat to live and they can eat only where the food is. They can live only on dead and dying tissue. If you want to remain healthy, then don't given them any opportunity at all to find their food in your body.

Ninety-eight percent of my patients have found that on the non-glue-food diet they no longer have colds or the flu or any sort of respiratory infection.

"I've been eating only non-glue-foods for a little more than 5 years now, Doc," Roger told me, "and you know I haven't even had a case of the sniffles in that length of time. But before that when I was eating lots of glue-foods, I used to get a cold in the fall and never get rid of it until the spring. What a difference!"

My wife and I can both vouch for the fact that when you don't eat glue-foods, your chances for a bad cold or the flu are reduced to practically zero. I can't recall when either one of us have had a respiratory infection since we've been eating only the non-glue-foods.

You can't lose weight by exercise alone

Some people want to substitute exercise for dieting. Forget it. You can't get rid of your excess fat by exercise alone. You must stop eating the glue-foods first. Once you stop taking in those man-made carbohydrates, some exercise such as walking will help promote the oxidation of your body fat, but not before.

Frankly speaking, I don't like to stand up if I can sit down and I don't believe in sitting down if I can lie down. I've never wanted to look like a professional muscle man. I'm a firm believer in taking it easy. So don't worry; you'll get no daily dozen from me to do.

I once had a neighbor — not a patient of mine — who did not want to lose weight by dieting. Ed liked to eat too well. He wanted to get rid of all his excess fat by exercise, specifically by running.

Ed was 58 years old and weighed nearly 225 pounds. His blood pressure was 210 over 130. He bought a heavy sweat suit and set a route through the neighborhood of 3 miles. Every afternoon when he got home from work on went the sweat suit and out he went to run on his route. He would come home drenched with perspiration, completely exhausted. Then he'd sit down to load himself up with man-made carbohydrates — beer, pretzels, sandwiches, etc. After a while he'd eat supper.

He lost about five pounds — mostly water — that way in a month. He was unhappy with the results and lengthened his route to 4 miles. I tried to persuade him to stop his running and told him he was going to kill himself if he kept it up, that some day his heart wouldn't take it any longer and that it would stop.

But he didn't agree with me. I went to his funeral last summer.

I thought of him again recently when I saw a television commercial of a fat man in a sweat suit, drenched with perspiration running to a sandwich shop for a big hamburger sandwich, french fries, and a cola.

Mild exercise is beneficial

I personally like to take long walks at a brisk pace. Walking strengthens your leg and thigh muscles. It helps your varicose veins, speeds up your circulation, and strengthens your heart. Walking also helps your digestion, your elimination, and your respiration. When you breathe more deeply, you take in more oxygen and you get rid of more carbon dioxide and other waste products. In short, walking every day improves your general health. *But it won't get rid of your excess fat.* So if you want to walk to improve your general health, do so. But if you want to walk to lose weight, forget it.

If you do walk, don't stroll. Go at a good brisk clip. But don't jog or run. Walk fast. Running and jogging, unless you're in peak physical condition, can stop your heart just as quickly and surely as playing tennis or shoveling snow.

How far you walk each day depends upon you, how much spare time you have, that sort of thing. But once you start, keep it up. You'd be better off to walk half a mile every day than go 5 miles a day once a week. I try to get in 2 miles every day depending upon my work schedule.

But I do want you to understand that I walk and participate in other athletic activities such as golf and bowling because I enjoy doing it. I don't do it to lose weight, nor should you.

To stay young at heart, associate with people who think young

Dr. Norman Vincent Peale is the best known advocate of the concept of thinking positively. His book, *The Power of Positive*

Thinking, * has sold millions of copies. It is a perennial best-seller and a classic in its own right. You can use the same kind of positive thinking Dr. Peale talks about in his book to stay young at heart no matter what your calendar age.

I know none of us can live forever, but I also know that a great many of us age much faster physiologically than we need to. Your mind contributes greatly to how old you feel and how fast you age.

A good way to stay young at heart is to associate with young people, or to *associate with people who think young,* no matter how old they are. The second of the two methods might be more preferable.

A person who thinks young is enthusiastic about living, he is interested in learning something new every day no matter how old he is, and he tackles life with the zest and curiosity of a child.

One of the youngest men I know is a patient of mine who is 79 years old. Mac is an accountant. He retired when he was 65. After two years of loafing and fishing, he gave up his retirement and went back to work. "The fish begin to stink after a while," he said.

Mac started a small bookkeeping service for small business men. He keeps their books on a weekly basis. He started small but his business continued to grow. Today, he employs two full-time bookkeepers, a secretary to run the office, and he himself puts in a four-hour day. "I'd work eight hours," Mac says, "but I like to get some exercise in the afternoon." Mac's exercise consists of 9 holes of golf, bowling, or walking. I just hope I'm that active when I'm 79 years old.

For a long time I fought against dividing people arbitrarily into age groups in our church school classes. I'm sure you're familiar with that routine. You know, if you're 21 to 35, you go in the young adult group. if you're 35 to 50, they classify you as middle-aged. From 50 to 65, they push you into the older adult group; and when you're over 65, they automatically

*Norman Vincent Peale, *The Power of Positive Thinking* (Englewood Cliffs, New Jersey, Prentice-Hall, Inc., 1954).

assign you to the senior citizen class where you can do your homework for your final exams without any interruption.

I finally got the pastor and the church leaders to go along with the idea of forming several adult classes based on subject material — not age — and letting people go to the class they wanted depending upon their own personal desires and what they were interested in learning — not upon how old they were.

It has worked out very well and everybody's happy, except for a few die-hards. By the way, since they've been using that system, our church school attendance has increased nearly 70 percent.

Another friend of mine, Bert Davis, sold his home and moved to one of those adult retirement communities in Arizona several years ago when he turned 65. Last fall he moved back here again.

"What happened, Bert?" I asked. "Didn't you like Arizona?"

"Sure, I liked Arizona all right," Bert said, "but I didn't like being separated from my grandchildren by 1,500 miles all the time, so last summer, Bob and Larry — they're my daughter's two boys — came to live with us for a couple of months.

"I'd never checked my abstract too closely on restrictions when I bought my house, so I didn't know there was a time limitation for visitors under the age of 16.

"The housing manager sent me a notice on the 30th day to get my grandchildren off the premises in 24 hours. Come to find out I could have them visit me for only 30 days a year — not a minute more. So I sold out and left. Let the old folks have the place; they're welcome to it."

Of course, don't get me wrong. I think it's a person's prerogative to move into one of those adult retirement communities if he wants to do so. I know some people who've done that and they seem to be perfectly happy and content to live where they do.

But housing developments that cater only to people over 50 or so just don't happen to be the thing for Bert or me, and if you really want to stay young at heart, I doubt if they're for you, either.

You can postpone old age indefinitely with
the non-glue-food diet

Scientists and doctors who specialize in geriatrics, the study of the special problems of older people, are constantly searching for new weapons to use in the battle against such ailments of old age such as arthritis, heart trouble, kidney disease, nervous disorders, respiratory problems, and so on. They tend to concentrate on the ailment rather than on the individual himself.

But in my practice I try to concentrate on the individual. I treat my patient as a whole person rather than as a disease to be cured. By doing this I can eliminate whatever ailment he has when I restore him to health through the use of the non-glue-food diet. As you will see in the next chapter, I've also been able to help my patients get rid of a variety of other conditions besides their excess fat by using nothing more than my non-glue-food diet.

When you go on the non-glue-food diet, in addition to getting rid of your excess fat, you'll gain back your good health, for your digestion will become normal, the absorption and assimilation of proteins, fats, vitamins, and minerals by your body will improve, your elimination will get better, and your circulation will improve tremendously. Your body tissues will become healthy and normal.

When you're eating the wrong kinds of foods — the glue-foods or the man-made carbohydrates — your entire body ages prematurely. Premature aging takes place as your protein-starved cells and tissues die out.

Your body cannot possibly use glue-foods to take the place of protein. *People who try to substitute man-made carbohydrates or glue-foods for protein age prematurely and die younger.* It can be no other way for that's nature's way of doing things. You cannot possibly violate a natural law without paying the penalty.

Your physiological age depends on your circulatory system

No matter how old your calendar years say you are, your physiological age depends entirely upon the condition of your circulatory system. Nowhere in the body is premature aging more evident than in the blood vascular system.

As I've already told you, there is a most definite connection between a disturbed carbohydrate metabolism — caused from eating too many glue-foods that contain sugar, flour, and starch — and premature aging.

Scientific experiments at various medical schools have proven that *people in their twenties who are excessively fat have the same kind of blood vessels as people in their seventies.* Their blood vessels have thicker walls and a narrower stream bed with resultant higher blood pressure.

If that isn't enough to scare you to stop eating glue-foods so you can get rid of your excess fat and not age prematurely, so help me, I just don't know what it would take.

7. Various health conditions improved by the non-glue-food diet

Fat people are much more susceptible to certain diseases than are thin people. They have a shorter life span. Physiologically, their bodies age faster. Fat people have more heart trouble, hardening of the arteries, and high blood pressure than do thin people. These are but a few examples. The list of physical problems that are caused by excess fat or that are complicated by it goes on and on.

As my case histories have piled up over the years, I've seen how many of these physical and psychological problems of my patients were either completely resolved or greatly improved as they got rid of their excess fat.

If you, yourself, have any physical problem that is either caused or aggravated by your excess fat, chances are that it will be taken care of, too, as you trim down to your ideal weight.

For instance, when you get rid of your excess fat, here are just a few of the other conditions that can be helped and some of the additional . . .

Benefits you'll gain

1. According to insurance statistics, you'll live longer.
2. You'll run far less risk of a heart attack.
3. Your blood pressure will be much lower.
4. Your circulation will improve markedly.
5. Your low nagging backache will disappear.
6. Your arthritis and rheumatism will get better.
7. A skin condition will improve — even for a teen-ager.
8. Your digestion will be much better. You'll be free from heartburn, acid stomach, gas, and constipation.
9. You'll no longer be short of breath.
10. Your sex life will definitely improve.
11. You'll not feel tired and worn-out all the time; you'll have more vim, vigor, vitality, and go-power to get your work done.
12. Life will become worthwhile again.

Now I want to discuss with you some of these physical problems such as heart disease, high blood pressure, low nagging backache, and so on, and tell you how your excess fat can either cause them or aggravate them.

I also want to tell you how my own patients have had these conditions eliminated or greatly improved by losing weight on my non-glue-food diet and how they feel now. But first of all, let me give you some definite and concrete, black and white . . .

Facts and figures about fat people and death

If you are fat, you will die at a much younger age according to life insurance statistics and mortality studies made by the American Society of Actuaries. How much younger depends a great deal on just how much fatter you are.

If you are a man and you're 10 percent overweight, your chances for dying before your time are increased by 13 percent.

If you are 20 percent above your ideal weight, the odds for your early death go up 25 percent. And if you're 30 percent overweight, your changes for an early and untimely death skyrocket up by 45 percent.

If you are a woman and you're 10 percent overweight, your chances for dying at an early age go up 9 percent; if you are 20 percent above your ideal weight, the odds go up 21 percent; and if you're 30 percent overweight, your risk for an early death goes up by 30 percent.

This increased mortality rate among fat people is caused mainly by heart failure, cerebral hemorrhage or stroke, diabetes, and such digestive disorders as gallstones and cirrhosis of the liver.

In these specific diseases, the death rate is higher in fat people

For instance, in people who are 20 percent or more overweight, death from heart disease in men increased 43 percent; in women, it increased 51 percent. Death from diabetes in fat men went up 133 percent compared to thin ones. For fat women, the figures climbed 82 percent. Death from digestive disorders (primarily gallstones and liver cirrhosis) increased the mortality rate in fat men by 68 percent; in fat women, it rose by 39 percent.

After a long term follow-up study of 5,000,000 insured persons, the Metropolitan Life Insurance Company reached these 4 main conclusions:

1. Overweight and excess fat shorten life expectancy.
2. Far too many people are overweight.
3. Weight reduction benefits fat people and restores them to normal good health.
4. There is a need to focus attention on the 25 to 40 year old group to educate people early and prevent them from becoming overweight.

So there is no doubt about it. The premature death rate is much higher in fat people than it is in people of normal weight.

If you are overweight, you have an excellent chance of dying earlier unless you get rid of your excess fat and unless you get rid of it right now.

Just ask yourself this one simple question: "Are you willing to trade 5 or 10 years of your life for a piece of pie or cake à la mode, a chocolate sundae, or a banana split?" Maybe you are; I'm not.

How excess fat affects your health

You've already seen that fat men have a death rate from heart disease that is 43 percent higher than men of normal weight and that the death rate of fat women with heart disease is 51 percent higher than in women of normal weight.

It really is no mystery at all why this is so. Excess fat puts an added strain on your heart. Let me explain that a little better to you by this simple example.

Suppose you had a little vegetable garden that you irrigated by using a small electric pump to move the water. Next year you decided to enlarge your garden. You extended your irrigation system, but you left your pump as it was. The next year you again enlarged your garden, but you still kept the same pump to do the job. And then one day the pump finally broke down.

What happened? Well, the first year your pump ran 8 hours a day, let's say. The next year it had to pump more water so it ran 16 hours a day. Finally in the third year, because of the great amount of water it had to move, it was running 24 hours a day.

And then one day it stopped. It broke down. It was exhausted. It simply wore out sooner. *The job you gave it to do was greater than its capacity to do work. Your heart is the same.*

Let me give you one more short example that actually happened to me. I think that will explain it even more clearly to you. One time I bought a used well-known freezer. It ran well for 10 months and then it broke down.

The repair man came, looked at the freezer, checked the motor, and said, "This is not the original motor that came with this freezer. Someone has put the wrong motor in. It is not the right size for your freezer. It is too small. No wonder it burned out.

"This size motor is built for a freezer with a 12 cubic foot capacity. Yours has an 18 cubic foot capacity. This motor had to run nearly 24 hours a day to cool your freezer. That's why it broke down. When I put the right size motor in, you'll have no more problems." And I haven't. The same thing applies here as before.

When you add pounds and pounds of excess fat, you must also add miles and miles of blood vessels to reach the extra tissue and to carry the extra blood that is needed. But you must still keep the same pump to do the job, for your heart cannot enlarge; basically, it remains the same.

Oh, it can enlarge just a tiny bit to compensate for the increased work load you've given it with your excess fat, but it cannot enlarge enough to carry the entire load. So to take care of the blood supply to your excess fat, it must simply work harder and longer and faster to get the job done.

You may not realize it, but your heart normally rests between beats. And when you increase its work load, it has to pump harder, and therefore, it should actually receive more rest. But it cannot. To meet the requirements you've placed on it, it has to beat faster than before, so it has even less time to rest even though it needs much more.

Your heart normally has plenty of reserve strength left to take care of emergencies. In other words, it usually has enough reserve capacity to handle the extra demands placed on it during heavy muscular work or hard physical exercise.

But when you overload your heart with your excess fat, you use up all your cardiac reserve; you now have none left to take care of any additional work you give it to do. Your heart is working at full capacity all the time just to keep you alive.

How do you bring about this added strain on your heart that causes it to break down? Well, you eat a huge meal — such as at

Thanksgiving or Christmas — or you get all up tight about something and have a temper tantrum, or you go out and shovel snow or indulge in some heavy muscular activity you're not used to, and *blam!* That's it; that's the end of the road. Your heart stops; it breaks down. Why? Simple. *The job you gave your heart to do was greater than its capacity to do work.*

What happens to your heart when you get rid of your excess fat

When you get rid of all your excess fat, the work load on your heart is immediately reduced. It no longer has to work as hard as it did before to get the job done. It has more time to rest between beats. And the best news of all: your heart will become normal again.

I've proven that time and again with patients in my own practice. When electrocardiograms and blood pressure readings return to normal after a person gets down to his ideal weight on my non-glue-food diet — and when no other treatment has been used — then the improvement in his heart condition has to come from the loss of his excess fat. There simply can be no other reason.

The American Society of Actuaries and the Metropolitan Life Insurance Company have also found that a person's heart returns to normal when he gets rid of his excess fat.

That has been proven by the blood pressure and heart studies they have conducted on thousands and thousands of people. Their findings show that when fat people reduce to their ideal weight, their mortality rates also become the same as the rates for people of normal weight.

In my own practice, I can't prove by any statistics that the death rate from heart failure is decreased in my fat patients after they get rid of their excess fat on my non-glue-food diet. That's impossible for me to prove. But I'm not conducting a scientific experiment; I have a private practice to take care of.

Besides, I don't really have to prove that point at all. The studies made by the American Society of Actuaries and the

Metropolitan Life Insurance Company have already done that for me.

Their studies show that when fat people reduce, their mortality rate decreases and becomes the same as that of people of normal weight. My non-glue-food diet gets rid of a person's excess fat for him. Therefore, by logical deduction, my non-glue-food diet decreases the risk of a heart attack and an early death for those who use it. Let me show you that even more clearly this way.

1. The loss of excess fat decreases the risk of a heart attack and a possible early death for you.
2. The non-glue-food diet will get rid of your excess fat.
3. Therefore, the non-glue-food diet decreases your risk of a heart attack and your possible early death.

How excess fat affects your blood pressure

The United States Army made a survey of 23,000 men and women to determine the effects of overweight. This study showed that among men and women of all ages blood pressure always increased in proportion to the amount of excess body fat they had. The army also found that high blood pressure was present two and one-half times as often in fat people as in those of normal weight.

Why do fat people have higher blood pressure than thin people? Because all that extra fat puts an additional burden on your heart and your entire circulatory system. There is more tissue for your blood to reach. It's as simple as that.

For all those extra pounds of fat, hundreds and thousands of more miles of blood vessels must be added to reach them. The only possible way your body can move the blood to all these new areas is to increase the blood pressure and to speed up the rate at which your heart beats.

If your ideal weight is 150 pounds, for example, your heart is also made in proportion to your body size, and it will be able to handle that load. But if you are carrying around 30 or 40 pounds of excess fat, you've increased the work for your heart and for your blood vessels.

When you get rid of your excess fat, your blood pressure will go down. I know that to be a fact. *I have never seen a single case in all my years of practice in which the patient's blood pressure was not lowered as he got rid of his excess fat on my non-glue-food diet.*

Patients who've come to see me with blood pressure readings of 180 to 240 have within a period of 6 months to a year on the non-glue-food diet lowered these readings to a range of 120 to 150 depending upon their age and the amount of permanent damage remaining in their blood vascular system. Of the hundreds of case histories in my files, let me take just one example, Armond D.

Armond's experience

When Armond came to see me the first time, he weighed 228 pounds. He was approximately 50 pounds overweight. His blood pressure was 240 over 130. He had a continual headache and a constant ringing in his ears.

Today he weighs 175 pounds. His blood pressure is now 130 systolic over 85 diastolic. He no longer has headaches and the ringing in his ears is completely gone. Armond gained all these extra benefits when he lost 53 pounds in just 7 months on my non-glue-food diet.

So if you're fat and have high blood pressure, take it from me. When you reduce, you'll also lower your blood pressure. It has to work that way for that's nature's way of doing things.

Arthritis and rheumatism are much worse when you are fat

Arthritis and rheumatism cause painful inflammation, deformity, and stiffening of the joints of the body. Science does not yet know either the cause or the cure for arthritis. Treatment in the majority of cases consists of treating the pain with aspirin.

But aspirin is not the harmless pain-killer that most people think it is, despite all the television advertising claims to the contrary.

Dr. Richard S. Farr, head of the Department of Medicine and Section of Allergy and Clinical Immunology at the National Jewish Hsopital and Research Center in Denver, Colorado, as well as Professor of Medicine at the University of Colorado Medical Center, is reported to have said that 10 percent of all the adverse drug reactions recorded in American hospitals are caused by aspirin.

Dr. Farr also says that one out of every 500 people who take aspirin experiences undesirable side effects such as skin rashes, asthma, and gastrointestinal bleeding.

If you do have arthritis or rheumatism and you are also fat, I will tell you this much for sure: You're going to suffer a lot more pain than if you were thin. You see, as your joints stiffen and become more difficult and painful to move, any additional burden you impose upon them increases the pain.

Once you get rid of your excess fat, you will immediately notice a great decrease in the amount of pain in your joints when you move them. And they won't be as stiff to move either. In those of my fat patients who have arthritis or rheumatism, I've seen the inflammation and the swelling subside, too, as they reduced down to their ideal weight.

If my patients are taking aspirin or some other similar non-prescription drug to kill the pain, they find they can either decrease their daily dosage or do away with it entirely as they get rid of their excess fat and reduce down to their ideal weight.

Bill's experience

As Bill S. told me, "Doc, when I first came to see you I was taking a dozen aspirin a day to keep going. Now I hardly take any at all. The most I'll take now will be a couple and then only on a damp, rainy day. Most days I don't have to take any."

Bill has lost nearly 60 pounds on my non-glue-food diet. He

works for the telephone company and spends 85 percent of his time outside in all kinds of weather. So you see, getting rid of your excess fat may not cure your arthritis or your rheumatism altogether, but it will sure lessen the pain and the discomfort for you.

Even your low nagging backache may go away

My inability to get rid of a fat patient's low nagging backache caused my interest in obesity and diet in the first place. I found that when a fat person with such a backache reduces to his ideal weight on my non-glue-food diet, his backache disappears in 95 out of every 100 cases with no other treatment.

"I think I'd tried everything there was on the market to help my backache," Charlie told me. "I'd put boards under my mattress. . . worn a back-support. . .took a course of special exercises to strengthen my back, but nothing seemed to help my backache until I met you, Doc. Now I feel wonderful. No more morning backache since I lost 50 pounds on the non-glue-food diet. In fact, no more backache, period!"

Charlie is one of those 95 out of every 100 who get rid of their low backache without any other treatment than the non-glue-food diet. Charlie lost 52 pounds in 8 months and went from 227 pounds down to 175. And as he just said, when he lost his excess fat, he got rid of his low nagging backache.

Now in the remaining 5 out of every 100 cases, there will be some other cause of the low back pain, perhaps a lumbosacral condition, a compressed disc and nerve pressure, prostate trouble, kidney inflammation, and so on. However, even in this 5 percent requiring further treatment, there will be a decrease of their pain when they lose weight. Although their low nagging backache may not be caused by their excess fat, it is most definitely complicated or aggravated by it.

You'll get rid of your indigestion, acid stomach, and heartburn

Glue-foods are the primary cause of indigestion, acid stomach, and heartburn. You will discover that on the non-glue-food diet, you'll no longer have that bloated and stuffy feeling that you get when you eat man-made carbohydrates.

You'll no longer have any need for those various stomach medicines you see advertised on television all the time. Heartburn and acid stomach will become nothing more than memories of the past when you eliminate sugars and starches from your diet. So will constipation. Every single one of my formerly fat patients with digestive disorders will vouch for that. Just like Donald F., for instance.

Donald's experience

"Doc, for the first time in 10 years I don't have to take an anti-acid tablet as soon as I finish eating," Donald told me. "I don't get any sign of heartburn or acid stomach any more. Nor do I belch up a lot of gas the way I used to do. And I'm no longer constipated either. In fact, since I've been on your non-glue-food diet, I've stopped taking any kind of pills altogether."

Just in case you're wondering, Donald's situation is not an exception by any means. Instead, it is the rule. So if you happen to have acid stomach, heartburn, or constipation, the non-glue-food diet will work wonders for you, too. Leafy, green vegetables, by the way, with all their cellulose and fiber, act as one of nature's best remedies for chronic constipation, if that happens to be your particular problem.

You'll no longer be short of breath

"Doc, the other day I left my car at the gas station to be serviced," Arch S. told me. "It was a beautiful sunshiny day, cool and brisk, just right for walking.

"So I refused the station manager's offer to drive me home. I decided to walk. Well, it's about two and a half miles to my house with some hills, too, but I made it in fine shape.

"Wasn't even short of breath when I got home. But I'll tell you one thing for sure, Doc. I couldn't have done that 9 months ago. Forty-five pounds off on your non-glue-food diet sure does make a lot of difference."

When you get rid of your excess fat, you'll be able to walk long distances again, too, without running out of breath. You'll be able to climb stairs without stopping to rest every other step or so.

Fat people are always short of breath. They're always huffing and puffing wherever they go. Their lungs are working overtime to supply oxygen to all that surplus fat tissue and they never seem to get quite enough to get the job done.

Most of the time, this is just annoying or embarrassing. However, if you have emphysema, it assumes a much more serious condition. And if you're faced with surgery, shortness of breath becomes a most definite danger to you. When you're going to be operated on, you have enough complications already, let alone adding still another one — shortness of breath.

Most deep anesthesia requires the inhalation of gas. For average people there is no extraordinary risk. But if you're fat, your lungs are already strained. Anesthesia increases that strain, and if you are so fat that you have no reserve lung capacity left, it could prove fatal. You could die on the operating table because of that.

Aside from shortness of breath, surgery is a greater risk if the doctor has to cut through thick layers of fat. Not only is the operation harder for the surgeon to perform, but your body will also heal much more slowly during convalescence.

Scar tissue cannot be created from fat tissue. Fat tissue will not heal and join with other fat tissue to close the incision. Only connective or fibrous tissue and lean muscle tissue can do that. If fat cells get in the way, the task is just that much harder for your body to take care of.

Fat people are not jolly all the time

Santa Claus may be fat and jolly, but you're not Santa Claus. I've never met a fat person in my offfice yet who was happy and jolly about being fat.

I've met many people who put on a mask to conceal their true inner feelings, but when the mask was removed, I've always found an unhappy, emotionally disturbed personality underneath.

For instance, a man falls in love with a woman because she has, besides her many other attributes, a good figure. She is good looking, attractive, well built, and so on. And physical attraction and sex are still the prime motivators of a satisfactory man-woman relationship if it's going to last. No man wants to marry a woman who looks like a fence post.

Then she becomes pregnant and bears his child. But she doesn't return to her previous ideal figure. In fact, she now has a lot of excess fat that wasn't there before.

The man no longer sees the graceful attractive woman he married. His interest in her declines. He spends more and more time watching television and pays less and less attention to her. Sex is no longer of interest to him, at least with his wife.

I have been unable to keep track of the number of fat women who come to me for help because their husbands have stopped having sex relations with them. And all because of their obesity — their excess fat.

One such woman comes to mind immediately, primarily because she was in my office just yesterday for her monthly check-up and she was glowing with happiness.

"I can't thank you enough, Doctor," Juanita said. "I know

you've saved my marriage. A few months ago I couldn't do anything right for Roy. Everything was wrong with me: my cooking, the way I kept house, the way I dressed, the way I looked. And our sex relations weren't. Life was absolutely miserable for me.

"But how different things are now. I got rid of 60 pounds on your non-glue-food diet and now everything I do is right. I haven't made a mistake in 6 months. And when it comes to sex and love, Roy acts as if I'm the only woman alive. How wonderful life can be when you're not fat."

You see, when a wife becomes overly fat as Juanita was, the entire home falls into chaos. The husband attacks his wife for everything else she does because of his sexual frustration just as Roy did. He criticizes her cooking, her housekeeping, the way she looks, walks, and talks.

Is it any wonder fat people are not always jolly? They live in hell and torment because of their excess fat. They become introverted and filled with self-pity. Yet there's absolutely no reason for them to be this way. All they need do to be able to enjoy life again is get rid of their excess fat.

The non-glue-food diet can prevent or control diabetes

If you are a diabetic under a doctor's care and you are already taking insulin, I wouldn't want you to go on any version of the non-glue-food diet without your doctor's advice and guidance.

But if you were to come to me before you had to start your insulin shots, the chances are nearly a thousand to one you'd be able to control your diabetes completely by the third version of the non-glue-food diet that is in Part 2, Section II of Chapter 3.

I feel absolutely sure in saying this for that particular non-glue-food diet version has been effective in bringing both the diabetes and the excess fat under control in every one of the diabetic cases I've treated, and I've seen dozens of them.

The smart thing to do is to take positive action before you

have any signs of diabetes. If you're carrying around 20 pounds or more of excess fat, or if your family background includes victims of both diabetes and overweight, you'd be wise to get on the non-glue-food diet in Part 2, Section II in Chapter 3 right now before it's too late.

What are some of the signs and symptoms of diabetes? Excessive fatigue, constant thirst, and frequent urination are common. If you have any of these symptoms, you should have your doctor run a urinalysis for you or you can do it yourself.

It costs very little to get a simple urinalysis kit at the drug store. *Clinitest* is a common test kit you can buy. You can check your own urine in a matter of moments. If the test is positive, you should see your family doctor immediately.

Fat people usually have poor circulation

Fat people usually have poor circulation, especially in the feet and legs and the lower intestinal tract. The lower extremities are farthest from the heart and once the blood gets down in the feet and legs, it's hard for your heart to pump it out of there.

That's why fat people end up with varicose veins and hemorrhoids so much of the time. Once a vein has lost its elasticity and has become varicose, it cannot be permanently restored to its original condition. However, getting rid of the excess fat will reduce the extra burden on your blood vessels and your varicose veins will diminish in size and give you much less trouble.

The itching of hemorrhoids can be most troublesome and embarrassing. But when you go on the non-glue-food diet, you'll find the itching soon ceases to be a problem. The man-made carbohydrates cause the itching. When you stop eating glue-foods, it stops, too.

I can most definitely vouch for that from my own personal experience. I inserted rectal suppositories day after day for years before I came up with the non-glue-food diet. But not any more. And I am not alone in that either.

"Doc, you know I just realized the other day that I'm not using hemorrhoidal suppositories any more," Mike told me. "I hadn't even thought about it for 3 or 4 months now. In fact, I'd almost forgotten I ever had any itching piles. Then I happened to see an advertisement in a magazine the other day for Preparation H and suddenly I remembered.

"Your non-glue-food diet sure brings a lot of additional benefits besides getting rid of excess fat, Doc. You ought to charge for those extras a patient gets, too."

Other conditions I've been able to help by the non-glue-food diet

I simply don't have the time or the space to cover all the conditions I've helped in my office by my non-glue-food diet. Besides the ones I've already discussed, I'd like to list just a few of the others that have either disappeared completely or diminished in severity as my fat patients got rid of their excess fat.

1. Skin problems, even for teen-agers.
2. Sore and aching feet.
3. Excessive fatigue.
4. Insomnia.
5. Sinus problems and susceptibility to colds.
6. Liver and gall bladder conditions.

So if you have any of the conditions I've discussed in this chapter that are either caused or aggravated by your obesity, then getting rid of them can be an extra benefit for you when you get rid of your excess fat. In fact, the non-glue-food diet will be just the thing for you.

8. What to do after you reach your weight goal

Almost all of my patients tell me they wouldn't allow themselves to get fat again under any circumstances. They enjoy the benefits of being slim and trim too much to run the risk of losing them.

I can think of any number of patients I could quote to show you how good they feel after they reach their ideal weight, but I've pulled just a couple of names at random from my files: Helen L. and John R.

Helen weighed in at 186 pounds when she first came to see me. She was only 5' 4" inches tall and she had a small frame on which to carry her excess fat. Seventy pounds overweight, she could hardly waddle across my reception room. But that was more than a year ago. You wouldn't recognize her today had you seen her that first time she came to my office.

Helen L. and John R.'s cases

"I feel like a teen-ager again," Helen says, "and my husband guards me as if I were one when we go out. Used to be he paid a lot of attention to other women at parties and neighborhood get-togethers, but not any more. Now he gets green-eyed if someone else asks me to dance with him more than once.

"And I can go to the beach again and enjoy myself without worrying about what I wear or what other people are saying about me. I don't tire out as I used to do either. I can work hard all day and still enjoy a night out now that I'm down to my proper weight.

"I wouldn't trade the way I feel today for a piece of pie à la mode or a chocolate sundae — ever. It just isn't worth it."

John feels much the same way. He weighed in at 236 pounds about a year and a half ago. He is 6 feet tall, has a large frame and should weigh between 164 and 184. Today he weighs 172, 64 pounds less than when he walked into my office the first time.

John's blood pressure was 210 over 130 when he first came to see me. Today it's 125 over 85, quite within normal limits for his age. But I'd much rather have John himself tell you the way he feels right now.

"A year and a half ago I felt like an old man," John says, "and I was only 36. When I got up in the morning I was more tired than when I'd gone to bed. My lower back ached constantly. I'd drag through the entire day, exhausted and worn-out. Weekends were spent sprawled in front of the television set for I was just too pooped to do anything else.

"But not any more. I bought a new boat and some water skis. Mary and I spend nearly every weekend down at the lake now. We also get some tennis in one evening a week and we've joined my company's bowling league.

"I have plenty of energy for my work at the office, too. In fact, I even got a promotion in the last year. The boss told me frankly he'd been thinking about firing me, but when I got rid of my excess fat, my whole attitude changed for the better and my work improved so much he changed his mind. Instead of letting me go, he promoted me!"

I have dozens of other case histories like these two in my files I could tell you about, but I think you have the idea now that it's a lot more fun to be slim and trim than it is to be fat.

If you do agree with that concept, then all you need do after you reach your ideal weight is to stay there. Here are several techniques you can use to do exactly that:

Take a picture of your new self

Now that you're down to your ideal weight, have a photograph taken of the *new you*. Have several taken, in fact — one at the pool in a swim suit. . .another in sexy shorts. . .and still another one in some of your new dress-up clothes. Get a close-up of your face in one so you can see how good you look without those puffy bloated cheeks and that double chin.

Will a picture of your new slim self motivate you to stay that way? Well, let's ask one of my patients and see what she says. That's the best way to find out.

"I had Ivan take some pictures of me in my bathing suit at the lake last summer," Teresa says. "The typical summer pose. . .you know, with one hand behind my head, the other on my hips, and a big smile on my face.

"Then I had some enlargements made. I put one up right along-side my old *fattie* picture on my dressing table. I put another one up on my bathroom mirror and still another in the dining room where I can see it every time I sit down to eat.

"Whenever I think — even for one little moment — about eating a piece of pie or cake with ice cream, I just look at those two pictures standing there side by side. That's all it takes; the desire to eat something sweet and fattening leave me immediately."

You can do as Teresa did, too. Before-and-after photographs will always give you a powerful incentive not to overeat again. One look and you'll be motivated to stay slim and trim.

Buy yourself a complete new wardrobe

Buying yourself a whole new outfit is both a benefit to be gained and a technique to be used.

First of all, it's a benefit. After all, you are entitled to a reward for your efforts and your achievement. So go all out. Get yourself a complete new wardrobe from head to foot. Go buy all those beautiful new clothes you could only dream about before. Indulge yourself; enjoy it; let yourself go. You've earned it.

Secondly, buying yourself a new wardrobe is a technique you can use to keep from eating yourself fat again. After all, you do have an investment to protect now, and a closet full of new clothes is a terrific inducement for you not to gain weight.

"I threw away everything I owned and started all over again from scratch," Vicki says. "I didn't try to cut down any of my dresses or my skirts either. I got rid of all of them.

"I even bought a slinky and seductive black satin nightgown, something I'd never had the nerve to do before. Jerry loves it and he loves the way I look in it, too. But I had to get rid of 50 pounds before I could wear it.

"It is sexy. I never dared wear anything like it before because you can't put a 176-pound 5' 4" woman into a black satin nightgown and expect her to look sexy and seductive. That's absolutely impossible."

So do as Vicki did. Throw all your old clothes away. Buy yourself a complete new wardrobe for your new slim figure. Then you can't afford to let yourself get fat all over again.

Don't eat any more of the glue-foods that got you fat in the first place

Remember the clue I gave you way back in the first chapter? Back there I told you not to try and *control* the amount of rich and fattening food that you eat. Back there I said, *"Don't eat any of the glue-foods that make you fat."* And that rule still holds true if you want to maintain your ideal weight after you've reached it. It's a simple as that.

Now I don't believe it's necessary for me to review all the forbidden glue-foods with you. If you have any question at all as to whether something is or is not a glue-food, please look back at the original list I gave in Chapter 3, Section I, page 72 .

Ninety-eight percent of my patients tell me they have no problem at all staying away from glue-foods to maintain their ideal weight. They feel the benefits they're achieved are far more valuable than a piece of pie or cake. As one of my patients, Leola, told me, "The taste only lasts for 5 minutes, Doc, but the effect goes on forever!"

However, about 2 out of every 100 tell me they still miss bread, especially at breakfast. "I like my eggs sunny-side up," Dave told me. "When you eat your eggs that way, you need one little piece of toast to get all the yolk off your plate. Have you ever tried to eat a soft-fried egg with a runny yellow center using only a knife and fork, Doc? It just can't be done."

Well, if you are one of those 2 out of every hundred, here's what you can do *after you're down to your ideal weight.* For breakfast you can have *one slice* — only one, mind you — of *whole wheat* toast.

You can also have *one-half slice* of *whole wheat* bread with your lunch and *one-half slice* with your supper meal, for a total of *2 slices* each day. And I do emphasize again that these 2 slices of bread should be *whole wheat.* They cannot be white bread. White bread is one of the gluiest of all glue-foods you can ever eat.

But that is the only exception to the rule of no glue-foods in your diet after you've achieved your ideal weight. Of course, if you do start to go up from your ideal weight, then these 2 slices of whole wheat bread must be the first to go.

Don't try to be a social eater

"Once you're an alcoholic, you're always an alcoholic," Carl S. tells me. "You're never cured. Every sober person in Alcoholics Anonymous is a *recovered* alcoholic, but he's not a *cured* alcoholic. There's a tremendous difference between the two terms. Actually, an alcoholic can never be cured. His condition can only be arrested.

"You see, a recovered alcoholic can never drink again. But he will never have any more trouble as long as he stays away from the bottle and as long as he doesn't take that first drink. If he does drink again, then within a matter of a few days or a few weeks at the most, he'll be right back where he was before. He'll be a helpless drunk, unable to control his drinking.

"But some people just don't believe this. They have to experiment and find out for themselves. They just can't believe that they're not cured. They feel so good after a few months' sobriety on the AA program, they think they can drink socially again and not have the problems they had before.

"So they try it again. But they always fail. They are never able to control their drinking; their drinking always controls them. The fortunate ones come back to Alcoholics Anonymous realizing they are not cured of the disease of alcoholism. The unlucky ones never make it back; they die in the gutter or the insane asylum, kill themselves, or become a wet brain — a living vegetable.

"You see, we alcoholics are like people with an incurable allergy. As long as we don't come in contact with whatever causes our allergy, we're okay. But the moment we do, everything comes apart at the seams."

You're the same as an alcoholic. You're a "foodaholic." An alcoholic is allergic to alcohol. You're allergic to glue-foods. If an alcoholic tries to be a social drinker, he always fails. He loses control of his drinking. If you try to eat socially again at your parties or your bridge clubs, you'll lose control of your eating, too. You'll always fail.

It's impossible to take one bit of glue-food and quit if you're a "foodaholic" just as it's impossible for a person to take one drink and quit if he's an alcoholic. Remember Irene R. and the box of cherry chocolates? After she ate the first one, she was completely helpless. She had to eat the entire box of them.

So don't try to be a social eater. Don't take the first bite of those glue-foods. If you do, you'll lose control, too, and before you know what has happened, you'll be fat all over again.

Here's a quick summary of easy rules to remember and practice

1. Don't eat any glue-foods.
2. Eat all the protein foods you want.
3. Eat all the fresh vegetables you want except potatoes. (If you go 3 pounds above your ideal weight, eliminate peas, corn, and beans of all kinds.)
4. Eat all the fresh fruit you want (unless you go 3 pounds above your ideal weight).
5. Keep on taking your vitamin and mineral supplements.
6. Use unsaturated oils in your cooking and on your salads.
7. Take a safflower oil supplement with each meal.
8. Don't go more than 3 pounds over your ideal weight.

What to do if you go over your three-pound limitation

If you follow these simple rules I just gave you *after you reach your ideal weight* and you start to gain again, it's quite evident that your pancreas is not completely desensitized yet. It is still trigger-happy. It is producing insulin the moment the natural carbohydrates from the fruits and vegetables you're eating enter your blood stream.

So if this should happen to you, all you need do is *return immediately to whichever version of the non-glue-food diet worked for you to get rid of all your excess fat.* If you take action as soon as you go 3 pounds over your ideal weight, it will take you only a few days to get back where you belong.

After that, stay on the version of the non-glue-food diet you're using for several months to allow your pancreas still more time to become desensitized and get back to normal. Then resume eating all the fresh fruits and vegetables you want and see what happens. If you go 3 pounds over your ideal weight again, simply repeat the process until your problem is completely solved.

It could be that quite some time will go by before your pancreas does return to its normal function so it can tolerate the natural starches in such vegetables as peas, beans, and corn or the natural sugars in such fruits as oranges, grapes, and apples.

And it could also be that your pancreas has been so sensitized in the past that it will never be able to be completely normal again. Perhaps you'll be one of the 5 out of every 100 who can never tolerate high carbohydrate fruits and vegetables again.

It just so happens that's my situation. I'm one of those 5 out of every 100 who can never eat peas, beans, corn, oranges, grapes, apples, bananas, or any other high carbohydrate fruit or vegetable. I must stick to leafy green vegetables and fruits that have an extremely low natural sugar contant. Evidently my pancreas was so badly damaged by glue-foods over the years it will never become completely desensitized again.

If that's the way it is with you, don't fight the problem. Accept with good grace the things you cannot change. Just be happy that you're not fat any more. The benefits you'll enjoy far outweigh the minor disadvantages of not being able to eat everything you *think* you want to eat.

There's an old cliche that goes like this: Eat to live — don't live to eat. When you live to eat, living can become really miserable for you. That, you already know.

But when you eat to live, life becomes really worthwhile, for then you can enjoy it to the fullest. You've discovered that secret. A great many fat people haven't. The key to that secret is in this book.

Index

A

Aches and pains, getting rid of, 19
Acne (*see* Youthful appearance, complexion)
Alcoholics Anonymous (AA), 23 (*see also* Fat, losing excess; Foodaholic)
Amino acids (*see* Sexual relationship, protein)
Aphrodisiacs (*see* Sexual relationship)
Appestat (*see* Glue-foods and Non-glue-foods)
Arthritis, 194-196
Aspirin, 195

B

Bacteria (*see also* Sickness)
  seek food, 177
Barbeque sauce (*see* Non-glue-foods, recipes)
"Beauty mineral," 177
Beer (*see* Glue-foods)
Beverages (*see* Non-glue-food diet)
Blood pressure, 19 (*see also* Fat, losing excess, health improved)
Blood sugar
  reactions when high, 49
  symptoms when low, 49

C

Calcium (*see* Sexual relationship, minerals)
Canned goods (*see* Glue-foods)
Carbohydrates, man-made (*see also* Glue-foods)
Carbohydrates
  energy source, 48
  surplus stored as fat, 48
  unnecessary, 56
Carbohydrates, natural (*see* Non-glue-foods)
Caveman's diet (*see* Non-glue-food diet, last resort)
Chicken Hawaiian style (*see* Non-glue-foods, recipes)
Chlorine (*see* Sexual relationship, minerals)
Cigarettes (*see* Vitamins)
Circulation (*see* Fat person, poor)

Circulatory system
  physiological age depends on it, 185
Coffee
  reasons to limit, 81
Complexion (skin) (*see* Non-glue-food diet; Youthful appearance)
Constipation, alleviating, 19 (*see also* Fat, losing excess, health improved)
Corn oil (*see* Fats, polyunsaturated)

D

Desire (*see* Fat, losing excess; Sexual relationship)
Dextrose (*see* "Glue-foods")
Diabetes (*see also* Non-glue-food diet, advice before starting)
Clinitest urinalysis kit, 201
Diet simplicity (*see* Meal-planning guide; Non-glue-food diet, advice before starting)
Dried fruits (*see*   Glue-foods)

E

Eating out (*see* Non-glue-food diet, advice before starting)
Eating pattern, 83-85
  eliminate glue-food snacks, 85
  establish sensibly, 83
  meal frequency, 83, 84
  snacks, 85, 86, 94, 95
    fresh fruit, 86
    at parties, 94, 95
    protein, 85
    sweet tooth satisfying, 86
  whenever hungry, 84
Eczema (*see* Youthful appearance, complexion)
Eggs (*see* Non-glue-food diet, advice before starting)
Energy
  from carbohydrates, 56
  fats a source, 56, 57, 58 (*see also* "Non-glue foods")
Enjoy older years to fullest, 164, 165
Eskimo diet (see Non-glue-food diet, last resort)

Exercise, 180, 181
  keep it up, 181
  mild beneficial, 181
  no substitute for dieting, 180, 181
  walking, 181

F

Fad diets (*see* Low-calorie diet)
Fat, losing excess (*see also* Non-glue-food
     diet; Sexual relationship; Youth-
     ful appearance)
  benefits to be gained, 19, 20, 188
  calorie-counting unnecessary, 33
  compared to alcoholism, 22, 23, 35,
     36, (*see also* Foodaholic)
  compared to stopping smoking, 25,
     26, 35
  desire as first law of success, 21-28
    conscious mind, 25, 26
    subconscious mind, 25, 26
  effortless way, 33
  eliminate cause (*see* "Glue-foods")
  emotional reasons to reduce, 21, 22
  first law of success (*see* Desire)
  forget problem, by concentrating
     on solution 34-38
    fattening foods, don't think
     about, 36
    ineffectiveness of fighting problem
     (example), 37
    think of benefits of being slim, 36
  health conditions improved (*see also*
     Non-glue-food diet; *also* indiv-
     idual listings as blood pressure;
     Fat person, death statistics)
  health conditions improved, 195-201
    arthritis, 195, 196
    blood pressure, 194
    constipation, 197
    diabetes, 200, 201
    heart, 192, 193
    indigestion, 197
    low-nagging backache, 196
    rheumatism, 195-196
    shortness of breath, 198
  how to find your real reason for, 26-29
  how to motivate yourself, 19-38
  know why you really want to, 19, 20
  not final goal, 20
  no-willpower concept, 35-37
  not necessarily result of cutting
     calories, 40
  one day at a time, 95, 96

Fat, losing excess (cont.)
  points to remember, 96
  success assured, 37, 38
  as technique to gain benefits, 19,
     20
  want to, not ought to, 21
  want-to reasons for, 27, 28
  weighing or measuring food un-
     necessary, 33
Fat person as alcoholic, 51, 53, 171
  (see also Fat, losing excess;
     Foodaholic)
Fat person as *foodaholic,* 23
Fat person
  arthritis, 194-196
  death statistics, 188-190
    blood pressure, 193, 194
    diabetes, 189
    digestive disorders, 189
    heart disease, 189-194
    Metropolitan Life Insurance
       Company conclusions, 189
    premature rate higher, 189
  not happy, 199, 200
  poor circulation, 201, 202
    hemorrhoids, 201, 202
    varicose veins, 201
  rheumatism, 194-196
  surgical risk, 198
Fats (*see also* Non-glue foods)
  polyunsaturated, 86-90
    corn oil, 87
    linoleic acid, 87
    olive oil, 87
    safflower oil, 87-90
    soybean oil, 87
    types, 87
Fatties Anonymous, 23
Fish Hawaiian style (*see* Non-glue-foods,
     recipes)
Flour (*see* Glue-foods)
Foodaholic, 36 (*see also* Fat person)
  allergic to food, 208, 209
  can't be "social eater," 208
  fat people as, 51, 52
  how to determine if you're one, 52
  not one bite of glue-food, 209
French dressing (*see* Non-glue food,
     recipes)
Fruits (*see also* Non-glue-food diets)
  juices, 75, 76
  when unlimited, 75

G

Gamblers Anonymous, 23
Garbage can example, 178
Glandular (metabolic) disturbance *(see* Glue foods; Non-glue-food diet)
Glue foods *(see also* Sickness)
Glue-foods, 44-56
  Appestat does not control, 63, 64
  to avoid, 45
  beer, 94
  canned goods, 47
  carbohydrates converted to body fat, 58
  as cause of overweight
    steps to eliminate, 46
  dextrose, 47
  dried fruits, 47
  effect on circulation of blood, 185
  eliminate (list), 72
  fat person as allergic to, 53
  flour contained, 46, 47, 48, 54
  glandular problems rare, 46 *(see also* Non-glue-food diet, advice before starting)
  how term evolved, 44
  how they make you fat, 48-50 *(see also* Carbohydrates)
  major cause of overweight, 44, 46
  man-made carbohydrates, 46, 47, 48, 54
    eliminated safely, 62
    example, 49, 50
  read labels to determine, 47
  starch contained, 46, 47, 48, 54
  sugar contained, 46, 47, 48, 54
  sweet wine, 94
  test for, 47, 48
  why everyone not made fat by, 52, 53
  why so many eaten, 54
Green beans with garlic sauce *(see* Non-glue-food recipes)
Glycerine and Honey Complexion Bar, 177

H

Heart disease *(see* Fat, losing excess, health improved; Non-glue-food diet, advice before starting)
Hemorrhoids, getting rid of, 19 *(see also* Fat person, poor circulation)
Hyperglycemia *(see* Sweet binge results)
High blood pressure *(see* Fat, losing

High blood pressure (cont.)
  excess, health improved; Non-glue-food diet, advice before starting)

I

Indigestion *(see* Fat, losing excess, health conditions improved)
Intercourse *(see* Sexual relationship)
Iodine *(see* Sexual relationship, minerals)
Iron *(see* Sexual relationship, minerals)

L

Low backache, 19, 20, *(see* Fat, losing excess, health improved)
Low-calorie diet, 39-43 *(see also* Fat, losing excess, calorie-counting)
  differences in food calories, 43
  energy loss, 40, 41
  fad diets, 42, 43
  muscle-tissue loss, 41, 42
  regained weight, 42, 43
  scientific experiments, 40, 41
    Georgetown University School of Medicine, 41
    Oak Knoll Hospital, 41
    Tufts University School of Medicine, 40
  Thermodynamics as base of traditional theory, 40
  why weight loss not permanent, 39, 40
Lamb chops Hawaiian style *(see* Non-glue foods recipes)
Lecithin *(see* Sexual relationship)
Linoleic acid *(see* Fats, polyunsaturated)
Liquor (alcohol) *(see also* Non-glue-foods; Non-glue-food diet, losing more than 20 pounds)
  not "glue-food," 93, 94
  watch mixers used, 93, 94

M

Magnesium *(see* Sexual relationship, minerals)
Manganese *(see* Sexual relationship, minerals)
Man-made carbohydrates *(see also* Glue-foods)
  "civilized foods" proven unnecessary, 60
Meal frequency *(see* Eating pattern)
Meal-planning guide, 117-145

Meal-planning guide (cont.)
  diet simplicity, 114, 115
  for "last resort" diets, 135-139
  for losing more than 40 pounds,
      129-134
  for losing more than 20 pounds,
      124-129
  for losing 20 pounds or less, 118-124
  snacks, 124
Metabolic (glandular) disturbance (*see*
      Glue foods; Non-glue-food diet)
  premature aging, 170, 171-173
    sugar consumption, 170, 171
    non-glue-food diet prevents,
        171-173
  sugar consumption, 170
  "trigger-happy" pancreas, 170
Metabolism change (*see* "Non-glue-foods")
Milk,
  reasons to avoid, 81, 82
Minerals (*see also* Non-glue-food diet,
      last resort; Sexual relationship)
  recommended products, 91, 92
  supplements to diet, 90-92
  trace, 164

                        N

Natural vitamins (*see* Sexual relationship)
Niacin (*see also* Youthful appearance,
      complexion)
Niacin, pellagra-preventing, 176
Non-glue-food diet (*see also* Premature
      aging, prevents; Sexual relation-
      ship; Youthful appearance;
      Youthful feeling)
  advice before starting, 110-115
    eggs, allergy, 110, 111
    eggs, cholesterol, 110, 111
    diabetes, 111, 112
    heart disease, 111, 112
    high blood pressure, 111, 112
    keep diet simple, 114, 115
    metabolic (glandular) disturbance,
        112
    when eating out, 112, 113
  benefits, 71
  beverages allowed, 80, 81
    to avoid or limit, 81, 82
  fat, losing excess
    author's experience, 69
    example, 68, 69
    quickly, 67, 68
    rate of loss, 67-68

Non-glue-food diet (cont.)
  harmless, 56
  health conditions improved, 187-205
    (*see also* Fat, losing excess)
    diabetes prevention or control,
        200, 201
  last resort, 106-110 (*see also* Meal-
      planning guide)
    allowable foods, 108
    alternating, 107, 108
    mineral supplements essential, 107
    no carbohydrates, 107, 108
    points to remember, 109, 110
    vitamin supplements essential, 107
  for losing 40 pounds or more, 105,
      106 (*see also* Meal-planning
          guide)
    alcohol eliminated, 106
    fruit eliminated, 105
    points to remember, 109, 110
    satisfy sweet tooth, 105, 106
  for losing 20 pounds or less, 67-96
      (*see also* Meal-planning guide)
    points to remember, 109, 110
  for losing 20 pounds or more, 96-106
      (*see also* Meal-planning guide)
    fruit "prices" (nutritive values), 104
    fruits allowed, 103, 104
    impatience considered, 97
    pancreas oversensitive, 97-98, 107
    points to remember, 109, 110
    rules added, 100-105
    rules eliminated, 100
    rules, general, 99-105
    satisfying sweet tooth, 104
    shopping list idea, 100-105
    vegetables allowed 100-103
    vegetable "prices" (nutritive values),
        101, 102
  major rule, 73
  modifications for personal
      differences, 98, 99
  skin problems helped, 53, 54
  teenagers, 53, 54
  postpone old age indefinitely,
      184, 185
  reasons it works, 64, 65
  summarized, 108-110
  why it works, 39
  without starvation, 70
Non-glue foods (*see also* separate
      listings *as* Fats, Fruits, Proteins,
      Vegetables)
  Appestat controls eating of, 63

Non-glue foods (cont.)
  author's own diet of, 48
  fats, 56, 57
    Arctic experiment, 60
    danger of eliminating from
      diet, 60, 61
    Belleview Hospital diet
      experiments, 61, 62
    E.I. Dupont diet experiment, 61, 62
    functions in body, 58, 59
    how excess stored, 58
    scarcity causes illness, 60
    sources, 57
  flour products eliminated, 45
  liquor, 93, 94
  metabolism change, 55, 56
  natural carbohydrates, 56, 58-60
    advantages, 62
    sources, 62
    no desire to overeat, 62, 63
  pituitary hormone action increased,
    55, 56
    effects, 55, 56
  primitive diet proven valuable, 60
  protein, 56, 57
    in diet, 60-62
    sources, 57
  recipes, 139-145
    barbecue sauce (Hawaiian), 141-143
    chicken Hawaiian style, 142
    fish Hawaiian style, 143
    French dressing, 140
    green beans with garlic sauce, 144
    lamb chops Hawaiian style,
      142, 143
    porkchops Hawaiian style, 142, 143
    Sukiyaki for beginners, 143
  re-educating taste buds, 54
  sugar eliminated, 45
No-willpower concept (*see* Fat, losing
    excess)
Nuts, avoid, 95

O

Olive oil (*see* Fats, polyunsaturated)
Overweight, major cause *(see* "Glue-
    foods")

P

Palpitating heart, calming, 19, 20
Pancreas (*see also* Weight, reaching goals)
  desensitizing, 97, 98, 107

Pancreas (cont.)
  stimulated by excess sugar
    consumption, 170 (*see also*
      Metabolic proccesses)
  "trigger-happy" in fat person, 49, 50
Pantothenic acid (*see* Youthful appearance,
    complexion)
Party food and drink (*see* Eating pattern,
    snacks; and Liquor)
Phosphorus (*see* Sexual relationship,
    minerals)
Pituitary hormone action (*see* "Non-glue-
    foods")
Polyunsaturated fats (*see* Fats)
Pork chops Hawaiian style (*see* Non-glue-
    foods, recipes)
Potassium (*see* Sexual relationship,
    minerals)
Potatoes (*see* Vegetables)
Premature aging (*see also* Metabolic
    processes; Non-glue-food diet)
  "protein starvation," 184
Problem solution not control, 34, 36
Protein (*see also* Eating pattern;
    Non-glue-foods; Sexual
      relationship; Youthful
      appearance)
  never becomes body fat, 74
  sources, 74
  unlimited, 73-75
Psoriasis (*see* Youthful appearance,
    complexion)

R

"Reaching bottom," 22, 23
Rheumatism, 194-196
Riboflavin (B$_2$) (*see* Sexual relationship)
Ridicule as turning point, 24

S

Safflower oil (*see* Fats, polyunsaturated)
Safflower oil capsules (*see* Youthful
    appearance, complexion)
Seasonings, 82
Seeds (*see* Sexual relationship)
Sex drive (*see* Sexual relationship)
Sex as pleasure not duty, 20
Sexual relationship, 147-167
  ability depends on what you eat,
    150, 156
  age no barrier, 164-167
    virility when fit, 165
  "aphrodisiacs," 155

Sexual relationship (cont.)
  athlete's example, 156
  attractiveness to partner, 165, 166
  cleanliness, 165
  fat, losing excess
    benefits, 149, 150
  if fading away, 147
  if improperly developed, 147
  intercourse as exercise, 156, 157
  lecithin source, 153
  minerals
    calcium, 161
    chlorine, 163
    copper, 162, 163
    essential in utilizing vitamins, 161
    important for power, 161-164
    iodine, 162
    iron, 162
    magnesium, 163, 164
    manganese, 164
    phosphorus, 162
    potassium, 163
    sodium, 163
    sulphur, 164
    trace, 164
  most important meal, 156
  Non-glue-food diet
    benefits, 149, 150
    effect on sex organs, 157, 158
    fat not problem (example),
      156, 157
    frigidity responds, 150
    grandmother's experience, 155
    impotence responds, 150
    quality improved, 154
    quantity improved, 154, 155
    saves marriage (example), 157
  as part of basic need for love, 147
  problems when fat, 148, 149
  problems widespread, 148
  proper approach, 156
  protein necessary, 151, 152, 155-157
    absorbed as animo acids, 152, 153
    arginine, 152, 153
    drive increased, 155-157
    six meals daily recommended,
      155-157
    stamina increased, 155-157
    tryptophane, 152, 153
  seeds and desire, 153
  vary love making, 166, 167, 168
  vitamins, 153, 154, 157-161
    A, 158, 159

Sexual relationship (cont.)
  B complex, 159-161
  B$_1$ (thiamine), 159
  B$_2$ (riboflavin), 159
  B$_{12}$, 159
  E for normal function, 153,
    154, 157
  E sources, 154
  natural stressed, 159
  niacin, 159
  others influencing activity, 158-
    161
  plan activities, 165, 166-168
Sexual stamina (*see* Sexual relationship)
"Sex vitamin," 153, 158
Shortness of breath, 20
  good nutrition prevents, 177-180
    body's internal disinfectants, 179
    bacteria, 178-180
    garbage can example, 178
    white blood cells, 179
    no respiratory infections, 179, 180
    glue foods and bacteria, 179
Skin (complexion) (*see* Non-glue-
    food diet; Youthful appearance)
Snacks (*see* Eating pattern; Meal
    planning guide)
Sodium (*see* Sexual relationship,
    minerals)
Sore feet, soothing, 19
Soybean oil (*see* Fats, polyunsaturated)
Soysauce, 141
Starch (*see* Glue-foods)
Subconscious mind, stimulating to
    work for you, 28, 29 (*see also*
      Fat, losing excess)
Sugar (*see* Glue-foods; Metabolic
    processes)
Sukiyaki for beginners (*see* Non-glue-
    foods, recipes)
Sulphur (*see* Sexual relationship,
    minerals)
Sweet binge results, 49, 50 (*see also*
    Blood sugar)
Sweet tooth (*see also* Eating pattern;
    Non-glue-food diet)
Sweet tooth control, 54
Sweet wine (*see* "Glue-foods")
Synanon, 23

                              T

The Power of Positive Thinking by
    Dr. Norman Vincent Peale, 181,
      182

Thermodynamics, (*see also* Low-calorie diet)
Thermodynamics, first law of, 40
Thermodynamics in human physiology, 40
Thiamine (B₁) (*see* Sexual relationship)
Think young
  associate with people who do, 182
  avoid age groupings, 182, 183
  interests not age, 183
  retirement community example, 183
  79-year-old example, 182
  to stay young at heart, 181, 182
Three-to-one-rule
  for faster weight loss, 79, 80

U

Unsaturated fatty acids (*see* Youthful appearance, complexion)

V

Varicose veins (*see* Fat person, poor circulation)
Vegetable oils (*see* Fats, polyunsaturated)
Vegetables (*see also* Non-glue-food diet)
  leafy, 79, 80
  lowest in natural carbohydrates, 79, 80
  potatoes major exception, 76-79
  seed or kernel, 79, 80
  when "glue-foods," 76
Virility (*see* Sexual relationship, age no barrier)
Vitamin B₆ (Pyridoxine) (*see* Youthful appearance, complexion)
Vitamin B₁₂ (*see* Sexual relationship)
Vitamin deficiencies, 160
Vitamin E (*see* Sexual relationship)
Vitamins (*see also* Non-glue-food diet; Sexual relationship)
  A and D can be toxic if overdone, 93
  B, C and E not toxic, 93
  cigarettes destroy, 92-93
  natural vs. synthetic, 91
  natural, how destroyed, 160
  recommended products, 91, 92
  supplements to diet, 90-92

W

weight
  establishing reasonable goals 29-32
    heavy frame, 30
    inches not pounds, 32, 33

Weight (cont.)
  medium frame, 30
  set intermediate goals, 30
  small frame, 30, 32
  willpower not needed, 33, 34, 35
  life insurance chart, 31
  reaching goals
    bread, 207
    compared to *recovered* alcoholic, 28
    examples of, 203, 204
    maintain with no more glue foods, 207
    new wardrobe, 206
    pancreas desensitizing, 210
    photograph, 205
    summary of rules, 209
    three-pound limitation, 209, 210
    what to do when reached, 203-210
Wheat germ, 154
Willpower (*see* Fat, losing excess; Weight, establishing goals)

Y

Youthful appearance
  complexion (skin), 173-177
    acne, 175
    eczema, 175
    healthy (experiment), 175, 176
    how to have, 174-177
    minerals, 175
    protein essential, 174
    pantothenic acid, 177
    psoriasis, 175
    safflower oil capsules, 175
    soap, 177
    sulphur, 177
    unsaturated fatty acids, 175
    vitamins, 175-177
    Vitamin B₆ (Pyridoxine) 176, 177
    niacin, 176
  fat, losing excess
    benefits, 173, 174
  key to, 169, 170
  non-glue-food diet to achieve, 171-173
    benefits, 173, 174
    example, 171-173
    methods, 174-186
  real "killer," 170
Youthful feeling
  key to, 169, 170
  non-glue-food diet to achieve, 171-173
"Youth vitamin" (B₂), 175 (*see also* Youthful appearance, complexion)